BURNS

HIS LIFE AND TIMES EXPLORED THROUGH TWELVE OF HIS MOST FAMOUS SONGS

GUITAR EDITION

BURNS

HIS LIFE AND TIMES EXPLORED THROUGH TWELVE OF HIS MOST FAMOUS SONGS

GUITAR EDITION

Douglas Robert Falconer

Other books by the author:

BURNS: His Life and Times Explored Through Twelve of his Most Famous Songs Arranged for Ukulele

as Doug Falconer:
Ukulele: Beginner to Brilliant Book 1: Beginner
Ukulele: Beginner to Brilliant Book 2: Intermediate
Ukulele: Beginner to Brilliant Book 3: The Blues
Ukulele: Beginner to Brilliant Book 4: Advanced (The System)

Ukulele: Beginner to Brilliant Books 1 to 4: Collected Edition

How to Improvise on the Baritone Ukulele

Copyright © 2020 Douglas Robert Falconer
All rights reserved.
ISBN: 9798578974465

DEDICATION

In loving memory of my father

Robert Falconer
(27th April 1923 to 1st March 2020)

Kind and generous, with a spirit of adventure.
Lucky to have you until 96 years old.
Mum and I miss you greatly.

CONTENTS

Preface: Robert Burns and me   xi
Introduction   xvii

PART ONE: AN OVERVIEW

Chapter 1: Robert Burns: Myth and Reality   1
Chapter 2: Burns and The Spirit of the Age:
    Romanticism   9
Chapter 3: The Vernacular of the Common Man   19
    Leezie Lindsay;
    John Anderson, my Jo

PART TWO: NATURE, LOVE AND SEX

Chapter 4: Nature: the Imagery of Love
    (1759 to 1788)   27
    My Luve is Like a Red, Red Rose;
    Ye Banks and Braes o' Bonnie Doon;
    Ae Fond Kiss
Chapter 5: Nature: Celebrating the Bawdy Body   61
    Green Grow the Rashes O;
    Comin' Thro' the Rye

PART THREE: POLITICS

Chapter 6: The Politics of Rebellion: Burns,
    Wallace, and the Jacobites   75
    Scots Wha Hae
    Charlie He's my Darling
    Ye Jacobites by Name
Chapter 7: The Politics of Egalitarianism   107
    A Man's a Man for A' That
    Auld Lang Syne
Chapter 8: Time and Tide (1788 to 1796)   127
Chapter 9: The Deil's Awa' Wi' Th' Exciseman   147

THE SONGS ARRANGED FOR GUITAR

Leezie Lindsay (Key D)	156
John Anderson, my Jo (Key Em)	159
My Luve is Like a Red, Red Rose (Key G)	162
Ye Banks and Braes o' Bonnie Doon (Keys C & G)	165
Ae Fond Kiss (Key D)	171
Green Grow the Rashes O (Key D)	174
Comin' Thro' the Rye (Key D)	177
Scots Wha Hae (Key D)	181
Charlie, He's My Darling (Key Gm)	184
Ye Jacobites by Name (Key Em)	187
A Man's a Man for A' That (Keys E & D)	190
Auld Lang Syne (Key D)	197
Postscript	203
Bibliography	205
Appendix 1: Converting Money	207
Appendix 2: Burns' children	209
Appendix 3: Important dates	210
A short glossary of Scots words	214
Index	218

A Note to the Reader

This book is for readers worldwide but, as someone once said, 'You can't please all of the people all of the time'. So, I have used UK English spelling throughout rather than American (e.g. 'acknowledgement' rather than 'acknowledgment'; 'recognise' rather than 'recognize').

I hope my editorial decisions will not upset anyone or affect their pleasure in reading this book.

Sources are credited in the Bibliography. Web page links work at the time of writing, but can be fickle and disappear over time, so broken links I'm afraid are beyond my control. However, they are not integral to the book and merely cited as sources.

The 12 songs arranged for this book are played on guitar by the author on YouTube *(hold down Ctrl and click the link):*

https://www.youtube.com/playlist?list=PLzqwFChU0wVn YgFHgNZJJDtnD2aa7doD4

Alternatively, use the YouTube search box and find my channel: 'Ukulele Beginner to Brilliant', then click on the Channel icon, click on the 'Playlists' and select 'BURNS GUITAR EDITION' to access all the videos of me playing the chord melody versions of the 12 songs in this book.

Preface

Robert Burns and Me

'Here's tae us. Wha's like us?
Damn few, and they're a' deid'

In 2007, nearing the age of fifty and having lived in self-imposed exile in England for nearly thirty years, my homesickness reached a peak.

That year Eddi Reader released her wonderful album, 'Sings the Songs of Robert Burns', and performed the songs live in a TV special. I was moved in a way I hadn't been moved by music for some years. It wasn't just nostalgia for my homeland; it was the brilliance of the songs and of Eddi's singing. Soon after, I discovered Deacon Blue's sublime version of 'Green Grow the Rashes O' on YouTube.

For the next few years I attended Burns nights every January (on or around the 25th, Burns' birthday). One unlikely venue was a seedy music club in the basement of the Royal Naval Association in East Street in Southend-on-sea where the English host cooked up a massive haggis using his Scottish Granny's secret recipe. There were various singers and guitarists performing Burns' songs through the evening and then a bagpiper in full Highland dress led a short procession of the haggis from the kitchen onto the stage, where an elderly Scot proceeded to recite Burns' 'Address to the haggis' as he ceremoniously sliced it open. We were all served a 'Burns Supper': haggis, neeps and tatties - and a glass of whisky.

Flashback to my childhood

For a kid growing up in Edinburgh in 'the Swinging Sixties' the zeitgeist was electric guitars, Elvis, The Beatles, The Rolling Stones, Carnaby Street chic, and Psychedelia.

Society was changing: the contraceptive pill was introduced in 1961; the first successful heart transplant was carried out in 1967; cinema films were appearing in 'Technicolor'; and the race for the Moon was on. Almost every house in the UK now had an indoor toilet, and by the end of the sixties nearly half the houses had a home telephone. Small, black and white televisions appeared in our living-rooms, equipped with indoor aerials that needed to be repositioned frequently as picture and sound disintegrated into fuzz.

Drab, post war Britain burst into energetic life: the economy boomed; girls wore mini-skirts; and boys grew their hair long and bought electric guitars.

Monaural records and record players gave way to Stereo and Hi Fi.

Psychedelic music and art were everywhere. It was 'the Swingin' Sixties' – it was a revolution in thought and behaviour, and Britain was leading the charge. In 'Lola' Ray Davies sang, 'Girls will be boys and boys will be girls/It's a mixed up, muddled up, shook up world'. Mick Jagger wore a dress. Keith Richards got busted for drugs. The Beatles and Donovan went to India to study meditation with the Maharishi. We were the children of Aquarius; we were 'semolina pilchards / Climbing up the Eiffel Tower' in a landscape of 'tangerine trees and marmalade skies'.

The world shrank. In the mid-sixties I remember going on holiday with my parents in an old plane with propellers. It took over 5 hours to get to Italy. At the end of the sixties we were there in 3 hours, travelling by jet.

By 1969 'the Space Age' was no longer science fiction, and on our massive new 26 inch colour television sets we watched Neil Armstrong take his first steps on the moon and Captain Kirk explore the universe in **Star Trek**.

Tomorrow's World (a British television programme exploring the latest inventions and predicting their impact on society) told us all, authoritatively, that we could look forward to a 4 day week and growing leisure time as we would soon have robots in every house taking over domestic chores.

We eagerly anticipated a Technicolor future of space exploration and unlimited global prosperity, built on unprecedented advances in medicine and technology.

In contrast, Scottish culture was an anachronism, an embarrassment. The most awful show on TV was a thing called, **The White Heather Club** which featured Andy Stewart, Kenneth McKellar, and Moira Anderson singing old Scottish songs with bagpipes and Highland dancing thrown in for good measure. The stars of **The White Heather Club** - laddies in kilts and sporrans, and lassies in long, frumpy dresses – were about as far removed from 'cool' as it was possible to be. They were throwbacks to an earlier age and seemed to have no relevance to a Scotland that was forward and outward looking, peacefully and happily wedded to England (the Scottish National Party, calling for independence, were a tiny minority then, and widely viewed as extremist cranks). Sean Connery playing James Bond, driving an Aston Martin with an ejector seat, and having an exploding briefcase, was cool; Andy Stewart, cavorting in his kilt and winking at the camera as he sang, 'Donald, whurr's yur troosers?' (Donald where's your trousers?) was not.

Burns had popped up occasionally in my Scottish primary school. I remember, at the age of ten, writing a poem about a deer (even though I'd never seen one, except in Disney's film **Bambi**) which was inspired by our teacher reading, 'My Heart's in the Highlands'. I recall another teacher reading, 'Tam O'Shanter'. We found it quite entertaining and got the general idea about the man escaping on a horse as he was chased by ghoulies, ghosties and the devil himself. But, to be honest, even for an Edinburgh lad, the language was mostly indecipherable gobbledygook.

Another familiar Burns' song was 'Scots Wha Hae!' with its lyrics about fighting and bleeding with medieval Scottish heroes William Wallace and Robert the Bruce. I always assumed (up until embarrassingly recently!) that 'Wha Hae!' was a kind of battle cry, like the 'Woo Hoo!' of Homer Simpson as he jumps in his car to head to Moe's bar for a Duff beer. I imagined the Highlanders, waving their broadswords aloft, and shouting, 'Scots Wha Hae!', just before they charged across some muddy field to be slaughtered by the English. I was rather disappointed to find that it was Scots dialect for, 'Who Have!' So the song means: 'Scots Who Have (with Wallace bled)!' But more on this in Chapter Six.

In secondary school, we read 'To a Mouse!' Some of the words were familiar – my mum often used the word 'sleekit' (meaning sly/sneaky), and when my silly childhood plans went wrong she would often wag a finger at me and say, smugly, 'the best laid schemes o' mice and men ...'.

But that was about it, and Burns vanished from my mind, a relic from a Scotland long gone and completely irrelevant.

By the age of thirty two I had moved to England and was working as an English teacher. The most popular text for fifteen and sixteen year olds was the novel **Of Mice and Men** by John Steinbeck which begins with a quotation from Burns' poem, 'To a Mouse':

The best laid schemes o' mice and men / Gang aft agley

Translated, this means: the best laid plans of mice and men, often go awry.

To a Mouse' is about the poet ploughing a field just before winter and accidentally destroying a mouse's nest. The ploughman poet empathises with the mouse's plight. However, at a deeper level the poem is a meditation on the fragile existence we share with all living creatures. Just like the mouse in the poem, no matter how well we plan for the future, the plough of Fate can come along at any time and smash our world to pieces.

Burns' respect for Nature and compassion for all creatures, even the lowly mouse, inspired Steinbeck. Setting his novel in the American Depression of the 1930's, he takes Burns' universal message and applies it to The American Dream. The main characters, George and Lennie, dream of having their own farm and living off 'the fat of the land' in order to escape the poorly paid drudgery of their lives as itinerant farm labourers. Their dream goes terribly wrong.

Many of the secondary characters in the novel also have dreams which fail to materialise. The novel is set on a farm, which is really a microcosm of America. Steinbeck is presenting us with a vision of a lonely, unjust society where women (represented by Curley's Wife), blacks (represented by Crooks), the old (Candy), and the intellectually challenged (Lennie) are marginalised and achieve nothing. Just like the field mouse planning for winter, the dreams and aspirations of these people fail against the harsh realities of existence.

Teaching **Of Mice and Men**, year in and year out, made me think again about Robert Burns. I knew almost nothing about him. What sort of life did he lead? What was he like as a person? What did he believe in? Why is he still loved the world over? What do these weird Scottish words actually mean?

Introduction

'Those who think that composing a Scotch song is a trifling business, let them try.'

(Letter from Robert Burns to James Hoy, 6 November 1787 – a year after the Kilmarnock edition of **Poems, Chiefly in the Scottish Dialect** was published).

Robert Burns (1759-1796) is the greatest poet Scotland has produced and, in a 2009 poll, was voted 'The Greatest Scot of all time' by the Scottish people.

As well as writing poetry, Burns took a deep interest in the folk songs of Scotland. He toured the country, collecting hundreds of old Scottish songs, editing, and reworking them into improved versions. He also wrote his own songs, setting his original lyrics to existing tunes and to new tunes specially commissioned.

His verse, with its themes of freedom, equality, and universal brotherhood has inspired people throughout the world, influencing the great and the good. Abraham Lincoln was an admirer and could recite many of Burns' poems from memory. Bob Dylan, when asked to name the song that influenced him the most, chose Robert Burns' 'My Luve is Like a Red, Red Rose'. 'Auld Lang Syne', perhaps Burns' most famous song, is performed throughout the world at special events and especially at New Year.

This book has five aims:
- to provide the interested reader with a biography of Burns
- to set Burns in historical, social and political context

- to explore the language and ideas in twelve of his best loved songs
- to present the songs in a format for guitar players to play the melodies with accompaniment, or as solo chord melodies.
- to do all the above with as light a touch as possible and avoid being overly dry or scholarly

A Note on the Songs

The songs are presented in the original Scots Dialect and also in modern Standard English.

The arrangements are in guitar friendly keys, presented in both TAB and traditional music notation: basic melody with chords symbols (suitable for duets with one instrument taking the melody while another plays the chord accompaniment; and as a chord melody for solo guitar.

The arrangements can all be played using a plectrum (pick) so no right hand fingerpicking techniques are necessary.

The 12 songs arranged for this book are played by the author on **YouTube** with some performance followed by tutorials.

If you have the eBook version: hold down Ctrl and click the link:

https://www.youtube.com/playlist?list=PLzqwFChU0wVnYgFHgNZJJDtnD2aa7doD4

Alternatively use the **YouTube** search box and type: 'ukulele beginner to brilliant' (which is the name of my channel), open my channel, then open the Playlists and choose 'BURNS – GUITAR EDITION'.

PART ONE

AN OVERVIEW

Chapter 1

Robert Burns: Myth and Reality

> 'God knows, I'm no the thing I should be,
> Nor am I even the thing I could be.'

Scottish actor Alan Cumming is to star in a new dance show about Burns at next year's Edinburgh Festival (2021), promising to expose the 'real' Burns and focusing on his poor treatment of women (he had twelve children by four different women). Cumming has this to say:

One of the things that I'm really excited about and really drew me to it was the seeming dichotomy between him being this man who was very egalitarian and spoke about the need for women's rights in 1792, so he was well ahead of the game in that way.
 Yet in his own life, in his personal life, he did not treat women very well. It is fascinating how we have dealt with that, how in some ways we have maybe biscuit-tinned him and sanitised him, and roughed off the edges.
 From the Edinburgh Evening News, 1st June 2020:
 https://www.edinburghnews.scotsman.com/whats-on/arts-and-entertainment/alan-cumming-reveals-how-his-robert-burns-dance-show-will-explore-poets-darker-side-2870615

Burns' life and death are surrounded by contradictions, mysteries and controversies. Let us now take a quick look at **the popular myth of Robert Burns** – the dominant narrative that was presented to me as a child – before looking at the probable reality.

Robert Burns – The Myth

In 1759, Robert Burns was born into a poor farming family. He spent his childhood ploughing the fields on his father's rented farm. The soil was so infertile that the work was relentless, back-breaking, and yielded pitiful harvests that kept the family in poverty.

Burns' farm labouring meant that he did not go to school. However, his genius was so great that he began composing poems in his head as he ploughed the fields during the day, writing them down in the evening.

He found a publisher and his book **Poems, Chiefly in the Scottish Dialect** (1786) was an instant success and catapulted him to fame. An Edinburgh edition of his book was published a year later.

However, Burns made very little money from his poetry, and he returned, disillusioned, to his rented farm in Ayr. He married Jean Armour, with whom he already had children, and had more children. To support his family financially he not only returned to hard farm labouring but took on a job as an Exciseman (a tax collector). He had fame but little fortune and descended into bitterness, drunkenness and infidelity. His evenings were spent not with his family but at social gatherings in town where he took full advantage of his fame by drinking and womanising.

Heavy drinking and overwork caught up with him and he caught a cold and was found dead near his plough in a freezing, wet field. He was only 37 years old. Other accounts say that he was found dead in a ditch after a night out drinking heavily. There are many theories about the cause of his death: rheumatic fever or tuberculosis for example; it has also been argued that his immune system was weakened through alcoholism and even venereal disease! He died a pauper, leaving his wife and children penniless and destitute.

I wrote the above account largely from memory, trying to honestly repeat the commonly accepted narrative of Burns life. However, I found it very close to the mythical view presented in this article, from *The Scotsman* newspaper on Monday 23rd January 2017, 'How Robert Burns died and his legacy examined':

HE WAS the humble ploughman's son whose ability to capture the Zeitgeist of 18th century Scotland through the medium of poetry and song carved a legacy which continues to shine bright two centuries on...The popular theory goes that Burns died from rheumatism having been found by the roadside in the freezing, pouring rain after a heavy drinking session...Scotland owes the Bard a huge debt, but the great irony is that Robert Burns died owing money - £14 to be precise.
https://www.scotsman.com/whats-on/arts-and-entertainment/how-robert-burns-died-and-his-legacy-examined-1457772

This only goes to prove the point that these myths about Burns (poverty and alcoholism) are widespread and generally believed.

Robert Burns – The Reality

The mythical version of Burns life, reinforced by the prestigious newspaper, *The Scotsman*, is not wholly accurate.
    Here is a brief and more probable account of his life and death.

In 1759 Burns was born into a relatively wealthy family. The top strata of Scottish society were the landowners, but next in wealth and status were the tenant farmers who rented the land. Burns' father was a tenant farmer. To rent a farm required considerable capital outlay and was beyond the reach of the majority of people who were peasants. Burns' father worked the land himself, but also hired peasant labourers. Burns, therefore, was not your average 'lowly ploughman' of myth.
    Although Burns family were of nobler stock than, or at least 'a cut above' the peasants, much of their wealth had been stripped from them after the 1745 Jacobite rebellion as Burns' grandfather, also called Robert (it was the custom to name the

first born son after his grandparent), had links to the Jacobites. Although Grandfather Burns gave no active support to their cause, in the aftermath he failed to sign an oath of allegiance to the king and was punished as a Jacobite sympathiser by having most of his wealth and goods confiscated, leaving the family so poor that his three sons were forced to leave home to seek their fortune elsewhere. Burns' father, William, went to Edinburgh and earned a living as a gardener before moving to Ayrshire and trying his hand at farming and fatherhood.

The family were well aware of their previous wealth and their now, relative, poverty.

Burns and his brother also worked on the farm, but it was customary in these days for children to labour on farms. It did not make Burns sickly, instead it turned him into a healthy young man, renowned locally for his physical strength. He also earned more than a peasant labourer and his income was at least average for the times he was living in.

As for being uneducated, Burns' father hired a private tutor and his sons had an excellent education. Burns' letters and poems are full of references to the great writers of his day such as Alexander Pope, as well as Shakespeare and Milton. In fact, not only did Burns have a sense of himself as being a class above but Mackie (Chapter 3 – see Bibliography) reveals that he was so well educated that his vocabulary by far exceeds every other British writer and is second only to Shakespeare's.

Burns' father sent him to Irvine to learn the flax trade. He was 22 years old and there he befriended a sailor, Richard Brown, some ten years older than him. The older, sexually experienced man tutored Burns in the art of seduction. In a small, tight-knit, religious community gossip travelled fast and soon he had earned an unsavoury reputation as a womaniser.

Brown encouraged Burns to publish his poems. The book **Poems, Chiefly in the Scots Dialect** (1786 – Kilmarnock edition) was a critical and commercial success and Burns enjoyed instant fame.

The Kilmarnock edition was followed the next year by an Edinburgh edition. Since the Union with England in 1707, and especially after the Jacobite rebellion of 1745, Scotland had effectively become a colony of England and the Scottish language and way of life were being suppressed and forgotten. Burns book of songs, eschewing English in favour of his own Scots Lowland dialect, was just the boost Scottish culture needed.

There are no definitive records of how much money Burns made from the two editions. Some biographers claim that he made very little, but Mackie speculates that Burns earned so much money that he became a multi-millionaire: in today's terms, Mackie estimates Burns' net worth at £3 million pounds, give or take a few hundred thousand (Mackie, Chapter 5). Other calculations, suggest Burns could have earned as little as £72,000 in today's money. I discuss money comparisons in more detail in Chapter 4 (and Appendix 2) but, for now, the truth is probably somewhere between, and I estimate Burns would have made something in the region of £1,000,000 at present currency values.

Burns mixed easily with the Edinburgh aristocracy (remember he was as well or better educated as any of them) and when he returned home to Ayr he was given a job as an Excise man, which was highly paid (in today's money his salary of £50 per annum would be between £75,000 and £100,000 per annum).

This kind of government job was often given to valued poets and artists as a way to reward them and keep them creating (at a time when Arts Council grants didn't exist).

Burns became a contributor to an ambitious project to collect and publish Scottish songs. In various short trips around the country he wrote down songs from the oral tradition in Scotland and improved them, altering choruses and adding his own verses. He was also involved in a similar project where he was given a collection of old and new Scottish tunes and asked to write lyrics for them.

Burns settled down, marrying Jean Armour and having children. He was in great demand, invited to and attending many social events in the nearby town but there are no reports of him ever being drunk. He was a sober and reliable Exciseman – so much so that within a few years he was promoted to Acting Deputy Area Supervisor.

Burns had a complicated love life. His first child was with a family servant. During separate stays in Edinburgh he made two other servants pregnant. Another child was the result of an extra-marital affair with a young barmaid in Dumfries. With his wife he had nine children.

Burns died at home, in his own bed, after several months of declining health. Contrary to the myths, he was not found dead in a ditch, or face down in a field. What he died of is unknown, but the most popular theory is that he died of endocarditis (inflammation of the heart).

On his death, Burns owed a debt to a local tailor, but otherwise left his wife and children financially secure.

In fact, as Catherine Carswell details (p.384), Burns' funeral was a national event, and considerable money was raised by friends and admirers specifically for the benefit of his widow and children.

So who was the real Robert Burns?

To a large extent, Burns created his own mythology.

Burns 'hoaxed' the Edinburgh establishment and although he was *'descended from a long line of tenant farmers and was at least as well educated as the average member of the gentry in his day… [Burns] represented himself in his first published collection of poems as a mere country yokel, and the ruse succeeded.'* (Grimble, p.12). Here Burns describes himself:

> The simple Bard, rough at the rustic plough,
> Learning his tuneful trade from ev'ry bough;
> …nursed in the Peasant's lowly shed…
> (from 'The Brigs of Ayr, a Poem')

This fanciful self portrait was picked up by the critic Henry Mackenzie, who described Burns as, 'this Heaven-taught ploughman' - as if Burns had been gifted his talent by Nature itself, drawing divine inspiration from the very soil he ploughed.

The image stuck. Hereafter, Burns was famous as 'The Ploughman Poet'. In aristocratic company in Edinburgh, he was not above playing the part of the rustic Bard to his advantage.

Accusations of drunkenness also appear to have been untrue (or grossly exaggerated). Burns was, to a large extent, at odds with the *mores* of the time. At the age of 25 he had been publicly shamed in Church for fathering a child out of wedlock and had a bad reputation as a 'ladies' man'. His many satirical poems and articles about the aristocracy and the hypocrisy of the Church, added to his unsavoury reputation locally long before he achieved fame as a poet. As part of his self-dramatising, he presented a rakish, hard-drinking image. Styling himself as a man of independent mind and something of a rebel, he identified with the Common Man and had revolutionary sympathies (as Romantic poets tended to, and which we shall explore in chapters 2 and 6).

The result was that there were many who were only too willing to attack his character and denounce him as immoral, a fornicator, a traitor, and a drunk. Adding to the image of Burns as a debauched libertine was the first biography, published in 1800: James Currie's **The Works of Robert Burns, with an Account of his Life**, 'presented a drunken erotomaniac whose excesses killed him.' (Grimble, sleeve notes to **Robert Burns**)

As for the debt Burns left, according to another biographer, Catherine Carswell, Burns' final farming venture had drained all his wealth, and in his last weeks of life he had written to various debtors and benefactors for money. However, it is more likely that Burns had a pathological fear of poverty, rooted in his knowledge of his family history, and his childhood on his father's unprofitable farm. His dread of poverty was no doubt amplified by his feverish condition. At any rate, his friends and debtors sent him more than enough money to cover the debt.

Whatever the truth of his final financial position, we do know that the myth of his leaving behind a widow in penury is exaggerated. After Burns' death a fund was raised that 'assured the financial security of Jean Burns for the remainder of her long life' (Grimble, p.123).   Also, Currie's book, despite being a character assassination, 'fetched a further £1, 200 for the benefit of the bard's family.' (ibid.) This sum would be, according to the UK government National Archives currency converter worth £52, 887.48 in today's money (a multiple of 44.0729. 44 x £1200 = £52,800). However, that is an unrealistically low estimate and a more accurate value is obtained by comparing either workers' wages, or *purchasing power*, then and today. A detailed explanation is given in Appendix 2, but by this calculation the sum of £1200 in 1796 would be worth in the region of £1,000,000 today.

While the details of Burns finances remain obscure, one thing is certain - Mrs Jean Burns was so financially secure that she felt able to decline a pension offered to her by the government in 1817.

Burns had his financial ups and downs but, by the standards of the day, he was far from poor.

Chapter 2

Burns and The Spirit of the Age: Romanticism

*'I'm truly sorry man's dominion
has broken Nature's social union'*

The **zeitgeist** (a German word meaning 'the spirit of the age') was encapsulated in one incendiary event – the French Revolution of 1789 – where the peasants overthrew the aristocracy and established a republic.

The revolutionary mantra of **Liberty, Equality** and **Fraternity** was a powerful new philosophy sweeping across Europe and threatening the stability of the 'ancien regime', the old order - the Establishment.

The French revolution inspired the most famous British poets and intellectuals, becoming a spark for the **Romantic** movement in the Arts.

Wordsworth's reaction to the French Revolution is expressed in his poem, 'The Prelude' (which he began in 1798):

> Bliss it was in that dawn to be alive
> But to be young was very heaven.

By the time Wordsworth wrote that, Burns had already been dead two years.

But Burns had blazed the way in championing, 'liberty, equality and fraternity'; he was the first of the Romantic poets, exploring the same ideas later found in the poetry of Wordsworth, Coleridge, Byron, Shelley, Keats and Blake.

Burns and the Romantic poets had much in common and here we focus on three points:

- a desire to use the language of the Common Man
- an appreciation of Nature
- liberal politics: an emphasis on equality and individual freedom

The Language of the Common Man

The eighteenth century had seen English writers take inspiration from the classical Roman writers. This period in history has also been called the 'Age of Reason' and the 'Neoclassical Age'. But there was about to be a revolution in both thought and style as fresh ideas took root in Europe. The new sensibility was a reaction to the over-intellectualisation of The Enlightenment. The Romantic Age had a new agenda: 'Reason' was to be subordinated to 'Feeling'; 'Intellect' to 'Emotion'; and 'artificial' language abandoned in favour of the natural rhythms and language of ordinary speech.

William Wordsworth (in the 'Preface to the Lyrical Ballads' 1798) stated that he wished to adopt **'the vernacular of the common man'**, dismissing the highly stylised language of the preceding Augustans.

Burns had already begun this literary revolution by writing in the Lowland Scots dialect. In a Scotland not yet wholly comfortable under the English yoke (has it ever been?), Burns was the right man at the right time. When Scottish identity was being repressed and eroded, Burns helped restore a measure of national pride by choosing to write 'chiefly' in Scots rather than English.

I hesitate to say that Burns gave Wordsworth the idea of using the language of ordinary people but there is strong evidence he did. Wordsworth was an admirer of Burns and his artistic debt is acknowledged in the book, **Land, Nation, and Culture 1740-1840** by Peter de Bolla, Nigel Leask, and David Simpson.

In chapter 10, 'Burns, Wordsworth and the Politics of Vernacular Poetry', Leask writes:

In his poem 'At the Grave of Burns', written during his Scottish tour of 1803, Wordsworth made no secret of his indebtedness to Robert Burns, 'whose light I hailed when first it shone,/And showed my youth/How verse may build a princely throne/On humble truth'.
Paying homage by adopting Burns' trademark 'Standard Habbie' stanza, Wordsworth evoked the Lakeland peaks of Criffel and Skiddaw visible from both Grasmere and Burns' Dumfriesshire farm at Ellisland, musing that; 'Neighbours we were, and loving friends/We might have been'.
Despite this homage to Burns, Wordsworth believed, on the basis of his reading of James Currie's 'Life' prefixed to his 1800 edition of Burns' poems, that the poet had died an indigent alcoholic at Dumfries seven years before in 1796. This explains Dorothy Wordsworth's comment, in her RECOLLECTIONS OF THE 1803 TOUR, 'there is no thought surviving in connexion with Burns' daily life that is not heart-depressing'. Reports of the poverty of Burns' widow Jean and his surviving sons 'filled us with melancholy concern, which had a kind of connexion with ourselves', she added. Dorothy registers familial anxiety concerning Burns' role as poetic ALTER EGO for her brother Wordsworth, despite the fact that of the two poets' 'neighbourliness', and their possible friendship, thwarted by Burns' untimely death.
https://link.springer.com/chapter/10.1057/9780230502048_11

N.B. odd grammar in the last sentence, but the general idea is clear. It is also clear that Currie's biography had successfully promoted the myth of Burns as an impoverished drunkard.

The 'Habbie Stanza' referred to (also known as, 'The Scottish stanza' and 'The Burns stanza') is six lines, rhymed: aaabab (the a lines being longer than the b). Burns used it often, as a flexible form adaptable for serious verse, satire and comedy. We shall see examples later.

Nature

Romanticism was about celebrating **Nature** and Burns was nothing if not a poet of the natural. Whether writing about a mouse, the bonnie banks of Doon or a red, red rose, the natural world is ever present.

In a time of increasing urbanisation and mechanisation, as people left the countryside and flocked to the cities to work in factories (Blake's 'Dark Satanic Mills'), the Romantic poets emphasised the purity and innocence of Nature. Romanticism celebrated the simple life of the country dweller, in touch with the natural world and uncorrupted by city life.

Nature as a theme was so powerful that it was often portrayed as a conduit to experiencing 'The Sublime'. At the very least, Nature was a catalyst for intense feeling, for an overwhelming emotional state beyond logic and reason. At the very best, an appreciation of Nature could be a path to spiritual enlightenment.

One of the most famous and representative paintings of the Romantic era is 'The Wanderer above the Sea of Fog' by Caspar David Friedrich:

This painting captures the very essence of Romanticism. The mountain peaks and tops of trees are shrouded in mist, suggesting not only the outer wonder and mystery of Nature but also the inner mystery of man. The figure in the picture is alone – a solitary, introspective observer.

To me there is something Freudian about the scene: the mist symbolising the subconscious and unconscious mind, and the mountain peaks the conscious. The peaks poking through are what we see, what we know, while the rest of reality is hidden, mysterious, unknowable. The painting is a reminder that what we see is not all there is. The figure in the foreground is experiencing the Sublime through Nature; he is communing with the Divine.

Throughout Burns' poetry, we connect with the natural world. We and the mouse are part of the same universal truths and laws. Even when comparing his love to a 'red, red rose' the simple lyric expands into a consideration of Time and the fate of the planet. We are one with Nature in its grandeur and mystery.

Liberal Politics: Individual Freedom

The third point that unites Burns with the Romantics is a shared political outlook.

As industrialisation progressed and people left the fields to work in the factories of England's rapidly growing cities, the Romantics looked back nostalgically to the simple, innocent life of the countryside. The common man, the rustic peasant, became idealised as a 'noble savage', born innocent but tainted by society.

Burns, a farmer and country dweller, identified with rustic life and with the peasant class. He saw himself as a 'man of the people' and disliked the social restraints placed upon him by the class system and by religion. As a Freemason, he valued Brotherhood, and the easy mixing of social classes that took place in the Masonic halls he frequented. His experiences in Edinburgh reinforced his dislike of the wealthy and aristocratic who, in some cases, regarded him as a lower being, a rustic zoo exhibit. These gentlemen and ladies asserted, or at least took for granted, their superiority over him without either intelligence or talent to justify it. Burns most clearly expresses the revolutionary idea of universal brotherhood in 'A Man's a Man for A' That' (see Chapter 7), championing the common man and ridiculing the rich.

Further, Burns was an unashamed fornicator. He saw sex as natural and good and not something to be regulated by the Church. His contempt for the Church's policing of sexual intercourse is best expressed in the satirical poem, 'Holy Willie's Prayer'. In it Burns (incidentally, using the 'Habbie stanza' mentioned above) adopts the persona of 'Holy Willie' (based on Willie Fisher, a church elder in Mauchline, known locally for his 'snitching' and hypocrisy. Here is one stanza where 'Holy Willie' confesses to God that he has had sex with a woman called Meg:

> O Lord! yestreen, Thou kens, wi' Meg
> Thy pardon I sincerely beg;
> O may't ne'er be a livin' plague
> To my dishonour,
> An' I'll ne'er lift a lawless leg
> Again upon her.

For the church to spy on people in order to regulate and suppress the natural instinct to procreate seemed to Burns to be wrong and the worse kind of hypocrisy.

Romantics and Hippies

The ideals of Burns and the Romantics are burned into our psyches today: valuing Nature; promoting equality, and championing individual freedom.

Burns would have felt very at home at the zenith of the 'hippie' movement in 1967, the Summer of Love. He would have shared the back to Nature philosophy, the expression of anti-establishment sentiments, and the pleasures of 'free love'.

The back to Nature trope found its quintessential expression in Joni Mitchell's 'Woodstock', fusing cosmic oneness (the Romantic Sublime) with the myth of Eden: *'We are stardust / We are golden / And we've got to get ourselves back to the garden'.* This is pure Romanticism, born of the idea that Man lost his purity when he developed awareness, or intellect, or Reason, and was thrown out of the earthly paradise Eden. Mitchell reaffirms our connection to the cosmos and calls on us to reclaim our lost innocence.

The hippies, like the Romantics, took the flower as a symbol of Nature and peace. There is an iconic image of a hippie placing a stem in the barrel of a policeman's gun as it is pointed directly at him. The hippie thought the flower would change the policeman's outlook; he symbolised a generation that believed they could change the world with 'flower power' and herald a new age - a utopia of peace and love. In 1968, the musical 'Hair' shocked the establishment and told us that this was the dawning of the Age of Aquarius and that 'peace will guide the planets / And love will steer the stars'.

Two hundred years earlier, at a time of similar upheaval and societal change, the Romantics celebrated the transformative potential of flowers and Wordsworth composed what is surely the first expression of 'flower power'. Here is the last stanza of his poem, 'Daffodils':

> For oft, when on my couch I lie
> In vacant or in pensive mood,
> They flash upon that inward eye
> Which is the bliss of solitude;
> And then my heart with pleasure fills
> And dances with the daffodils.

Wordsworth's 'inward eye' is a clue to the Romantic philosophy: the secrets of the universe are to be found not in science and reason but in experiencing Nature and gazing inwards. This introspection was assisted by drugs: laudanum and opiates were commonly used medicines but they were also taken extensively by poets in search of transcendent experience; the most famous opium-fuelled poem being Coleridge's 'Kubla Khan', which he imagined in a narcotic haze.

Two hundred years later, the hippies were experimenting with drugs for similar reasons – to transcend the material, to experience the Sublime, to access the ultimate reality and commune with the Infinite. The Doors, led by the visionary poet Jim Morrison, took their name from William Blake:

if the doors of perception were cleansed every thing would appear to man as it is, infinite.

Burns' 'flower power' was of a different order, and if there was any kind of addiction involved it was sexual rather than narcotic. His delight in Nature was joyous but it was earthy rather than introspective and transcendent. In his songs and poems Nature is often closely linked to one specific natural activity – sex. Burns drew on natural imagery to mix the high and the low, the sentimental and the bawdy, the physical and the spiritual, the profane and the sacred, the serious and the humorous. The Romantics saw Nature as a gateway to the Sublime, but for Burns, sex was sublime.

In the following poem (writing in English this time, as opposed to Scots vernacular) Burns mixes Nature with sex and humour in a way that is characteristically his (and possibly unique among the Romantic poets, with the exception of Lord Byron, who shared Burns' libertine inclinations):

On A Bank Of Flowers

On a bank of flowers, in a summer day,
For summer lightly drest,
The youthful, blooming Nelly lay,
With love and sleep opprest;
When Willie, wand'ring thro' the wood,
Who for her favour oft had sued;

He gaz'd, he wish'd
He fear'd, he blush'd,
And trembled where he stood.

Her closed eyes, like weapons sheath'd,
Were seal'd in soft repose;
Her lip, still as she fragrant breath'd,
It richer dyed the rose;
The springing lilies, sweetly prest,
Wild-wanton kissed her rival breast;
He gaz'd, he wish'd,
He fear'd, he blush'd,
His bosom ill at rest.

Her robes, light-waving in the breeze,
Her tender limbs embrace;
Her lovely form, her native ease,
All harmony and grace;
Tumultuous tides his pulses roll,
A faltering, ardent kiss he stole;
He gaz'd, he wish'd,
He fear'd, he blush'd,
And sigh'd his very soul.

As flies the partridge from the brake,
On fear-inspired wings,
So Nelly, starting, half-awake,
Away affrighted springs ;
But Willie follow'd -- as he should,
He overtook her in the wood;
He vow'd, he pray'd,
He found the maid
Forgiving all, and good.

(published in **The Scots Musical Museum**, 1790)

CHAPTER 3

The Vernacular of the Common Man

'Leezie Lindsay'
'John Anderson, my Jo'

Some hae meat and canna eat,
And some wad eat that want it,
But we hae meat and we can eat,
And sae the Lord be thankit.
(Burns, 'the Selkirk Grace')

Vernacular simply means the language and dialect spoken by the people in a particular region. Dialects deviate from the standard in having their own grammatical rules and unique vocabulary. Scots English is a distinct dialect of English in the way that Yorkshire or Geordie or any other dialect is distinct.

After the success of **Poems Chiefly in the Scottish Dialect (Edinburgh edition, 1787)** Burns was approached by a man called James Johnson who was collecting old Scots songs and publishing them with piano arrangements. Burns became a keen contributor and in the next few years embarked on various short tours around different parts of Scotland, usually with a male companion, enthusiastically seeking and writing down the songs he encountered. On his tours he was wined and dined by aristocrats keen to meet the 'Ploughman Poet' now hailed as Scotland's Bard.

Song writing was to occupy much of his creative output for the remaining 9 years of his life and he contributed approximately 370 songs (McIntyre, p.449). Many were of his own invention and the rest were found songs which he, to varying extents, reworked and improved. The songs appeared in various editions of Johnson's **The Scots Musical Museum**. To the 3rd edition, 1790, Burns contributed 'John Anderson, my Jo' and some Jacobite songs. The 4th edition, 1792, was two-thirds penned by Burns and contained, 'The Bonnie Banks O'Doon' and 'A Parcel O'Rogues'.

In 1792 Burns was asked by another editor, George Thomson, if he would contribute to a new, upmarket songbook. The first volume of **A Select Collection: Original Scottish Airs** was published in 1793, and contained 25 songs, six by Burns. The same year Burns wrote 'Scots Wha Hae' and 'My Love is Like a Red, Red Rose'.

After the Union of 1707, the official written language of Scotland - used in religion, education, the courts, and government - was Standard English. Much of Scotland still spoke exclusively Gaelic but that language, along with Scottish English dialects, was subordinated – merely, the languages of the peasants, having little prestige and in danger of extinction. However, Burns (who spoke and wrote perfectly well in English) decided to revive the Lowland Scots dialect with his book **Poems; Chiefly in the Scottish Dialect (1786)**.

Some critics have cast doubt on whether the dialect he writes in resembled at all the language spoken by his native Scots. Having a grandmother from Hamilton, I can assure you it does.

Another strong reason for Burns' decision to adopt the vernacular of the common Scot is his strong admiration for the poet Robert Fergusson, who died at the age of 24 in an insane asylum in Edinburgh. Fergusson wrote in Scots dialect and Burns emulated him, absorbing some elements of Fergusson's style.

Burns acknowledged his debt when he called him, my 'elder brother in misfortune, by far my elder brother in the muse' and commissioned and paid for a headstone for Fergusson's grave in the Canongate Churchyard in Edinburgh.

For our first song we have a very, very gentle introduction to the Lowland Scots Dialect. Here is one of the shortest and simplest lyrics. It was found by Burns as he travelled throughout Scotland collecting songs for Johnson's book. It is only four short lines but has a pleasing and popular tune.

Leezie Lindsay

Original Lowland Scots	Modern Translation
Will ye go to the Hielands, Leezie Lindsay, Will ye go to the Hielands wi' me? Will ye go to the Hielands, Leezie Lindsay, My pride and my darling to be.	Will you go to the Highlands, Lizzie Lindsay, Will you go to the Highlands with me? Will you go to the Highlands, Lizzie Lindsay, My pride and my darling to be.

Commentary

As we can see Lowland Scots here only has a few subtle differences to the Standard English used in the modern translation: 'Leezie' is the Scots pronunciation of 'Lizzie' (the diminutive of Elizabeth); 'ye' is the dialect word for 'you'; 'wi' means 'with', and 'Hielands' (pronounced 'Heelands') is an alternative spelling of 'Highlands' which conveys the Lowland Scots accent.

This lyric is described as 'a fragment' and this is all Burns gives us of a longer, traditional song, with different versions. Leezie Lindsay is the name of a girl courted by a Highland Laird (Lord) who asks her to leave Edinburgh and go to the Highlands with him. She is eventually persuaded to go and the song has a happy ending as they get married and she becomes the lady of a great castle.

John Anderson, my Jo

Here is a slightly more challenging song from the point of view of understanding the Lowland Scots vernacular.

Try reading the original first and work out what the words mean (some are just phonetic spellings of familiar English words in order to capture the Scots accent, but others are dialect words not used in Standard English).

Original Lowland Scots	Translation into Modern Standard English
John Anderson, my jo, John, When we were first acquent, Your locks were like the raven, Your bonnie brow was brent; But now your brow is beld, John, Your locks are like the snaw; But blessings on your frosty pow, John Anderson, my jo.	John Anderson, my sweetheart, John, When we were first acquainted, Your locks were like the raven, Your handsome brow was smooth; But now your brow is bald, John, Your locks are like the snow; But blessings on your white head, John Anderson, my sweetheart.
John Anderson, my jo, John, We clamb the hill thegither; And monie a cantie day, John, We've had wi' ane anither; Now we maun totter down, John And hand in hand we'll go, And sleep thegither at the foot, John Anderson, my jo.	John Anderson, my sweetheart, John, We climbed the hill together; And many a cheerful day, John, We've had with one another; Now we must stagger down, John And hand in hand we'll go, And sleep together at the foot, John Anderson, my sweetheart.

Glossary:
Jo = sweetheart
Acquent = acquainted
Locks = hair

Brent = smooth
Beld = bald
Snaw = snow
Frosty pow = white head
Cantie = lively, cheerful, pleasant,

Commentary

The speaker of the poem is an old woman, Mrs Anderson, addressing her husband, John Anderson.

The first puzzle is the meaning of 'jo' in the first line. It is Lowland Scots for 'sweetheart'.

The narrator is speaking to John, telling him that when they first met his hair was as black as a raven and his youthful brow was smooth (unwrinkled). Now his hair is thinning, and his black hair has turned white. Burns uses the metaphor of snow and then frost to suggest not just the whiteness but to link the aging process to the seasons: the lovers are now in the winter of their life.

The second stanza makes clear that where once they climbed up and down the hill together, now they are so old they can only 'totter' down - a wonderful word capturing the infirmity of old age.

The last few images of them descending the hill 'hand in hand' to 'sleep' together at the foot of the hill is a touching affirmation of love. Sleep is a gentle metaphor for death and she is telling him that they will face death together at the end of their long happy life.

The song had existed long before Burns in a bawdy (rude) version. However, Burns rewrote it into a tender love song. It may also have been his tribute to a real John Anderson, a carpenter, who was a contemporary and friend, rumoured to have built Burns' coffin.

PART TWO

NATURE, LOVE AND SEX

Chapter 4

Nature: the Imagery of Love

(1759 to 1788)

'My Love is like a Red, Red, Rose'
'Ye Banks and Braes o'Bonnie Doon'
'Ae Fond Kiss'

'Gie me ae spark o' Nature's fire,
That's a' the learning I desire'

Childhood and Youth (1759 to 1780)

Imagine you are Robert Burns, born in 1759, to William and Agnes Burness (it would be some years before the spelling was changed to Burns). You spend your childhood in the 1760's living and working on your father's farm at Mount Oliphant, near Alloway, in south west Scotland. During the week you labour in the fields and on Sundays you go to church, not because your father is religious (although he is – very), but because everyone did back then, and the church kept a register. You probably love going because it is one of the few opportunities you get to meet people outside your immediate family.

As the 1760's roll into the 1770's and you pass puberty you are partnered in the summer with a girl around your age (15) to harvest the crops. She sings, with the sweetest voice, as she works. There the two of you are, sharing that intimate connection with the land, breathing the fresh country air deep into your lungs, toiling in harmony with each other and in tune with the very rhythms of Nature. You talk and joke together and, as the day wanes, share the magical twilight when the sun casts a golden glow over the fecund fields.

If that isn't a recipe for sexual desire, I don't know what is.

If you haven't read it I recommend D H Lawrence's **The Rainbow** – just the first page will do – he makes farming the sexiest thing in the world.

So, it is no wonder that Burns earliest recorded amour was Nelly Kirkpatrick, his harvesting partner when he was fifteen years old. It was an innocent infatuation, as you might expect, involving young people brought up in such isolated conditions with limited opportunities to interact with the opposite sex.

In the summer of 1775 Burns had his second innocent infatuation. His father sent him to brush up on his Maths at a summer school in Kirkoswald. From the classroom window he saw Peggy Thomson and fell in love.

It was a short lived pang of youthful, innocent desire and Burns soon returned to the isolation of the farm.

In 1776, William Burness gave up the millstone of Mount Oliphant farm, and took over the tenancy of 130 acre Lochlea farm near the town of Tarbolton. Not only did the prosperity of the family improve, but Robert Burns' social horizons expanded. He befriended David Sillar and the two would often go long walks together on a Sunday after church. When they met girls on their rambles Sillar was impressed by how easily Burns could strike up a conversation with them.

Sillar describes Burns appearance:

He wore the only tied hair in the parish; and in the church, his plaid, which was of a particular colour, I think, fillemot, he wrapped in a particular manner round his shoulders. (McIntyre, p. 34)

Burns' unique, flamboyant hairstyle would have made him stand out in a small, rural community where conformity was high. Burns, like a true Romantic poet, was not above making a fashion statement to signal his non-conformity. He was hardly a teenage rebel (more a loyal and hard working son) but, at the age of 18, he upset his father, William, when he attended a dancing school in Tarbolton. William, a deeply religious man, had forbidden this and Burns always regretted the rift it caused between them.

Burns' third infatuation happened soon after: he proposed marriage to Alison Begbie, but she declined his offer.

While women were clearly becoming an interest, Burns did not entirely surrender to his libido. With his friend David Sillar he formed the Tarbolton Bachelor Club in 1780 for the purposes of debating the topics of the day, such as 'Whether is the savage man, or the peasant of a civilized country, in the most happy situation?' It is believed that Burns authored the rules for the club:

Every man proper for a member of this society must have a frank, honest, open heart' above anything dirty or mean, & must be a professed lover of one or more of the female sex. (Grimble,p.27)

It was in the Tarbolton Bachelor Club that Burns honed his skills of arguing and debating and established a reputation for his oratory.

Freemasonry, Flax and Free Love (1781 to 1784)

In 1781, Burns was inducted into the St. David's Lodge of Tarbolton and became a Freemason. Today, many conspiracy theories surround Freemasonry, but in Burns' time it was widespread in Scotland and, to my knowledge, had no sinister undertones but operated very much like a gentleman's club, comparable to the modern day Rotary Club.

Many biographers ignore or downplay Burns' masonic connections, leaving the impression that he was not overly involved and unlikely to have progressed beyond the lowest levels. However, Crawford (p. 111) reveals that Burns reached the rank of Deputy Master of St. James Lodge, Tarbolton and regularly attended this and other Lodges, including Edinburgh, where he made important contacts. I think it would be straying too far into the terrain of conspiracy theorists to see this as negative or harmful. Crawford argues that Freemasonry influenced Burns positively, helping to develop his desire for self-improvement and good fellowship. Freemasonry promoted the virtues of: 'Freedom, Harmony and Love' (Crawford, p.112). The Masonic world developed Burns' democratic leanings: here the rich and poor could mix freely and call each other 'Brother'. As we shall see in Chapter 7, ideas of democracy and brotherhood permeate Burns' work and perhaps these ideas came from Freemasonry as much as from his own temperament, and the French revolution.

The same year, 1781, the twenty two year old Burns was sent by his father to Irvine to learn the profitable flax trade (processing flax into linen had become a growth industry). With a partner he opened a 'shop' for the processing of flax. Celebrating New Year in the premises, the partner's wife, no doubt gloriously drunk, knocked over a lighted candle, starting a fire that burned the shop down. No one was injured but that was the end of the flax business.

Burns stayed on in Irvine, which was one of the most important ports in the country.

It's an old, familiar story: the young farm boy getting his first taste of the big, sinful city – and liking it. He frequented the book shops, stimulating his imagination, and it was here that he probably read the poet Robert Fergusson, who greatly influenced his poetic style. He also befriended an older man, a sailor called Richard Brown, who had a 'love them and leave them' philosophy and was Burns' mentor in the art of seduction.

Further, Carswell reveals that Irvine became the land of erotic opportunity that year. A woman preacher, Elizabeth Buchan (Elspeth Buchan, according to Crawford, p.115), appeared on the scene:

> She preached free love with fervour and dispensed absolution for all moral lapses.
> (Carswell, p. 98).

The religious cult she was part of became popular with women and Burns became 'acquainted with a follower named Jean Gardner.' (ibid. p.98). Jean tried to persuade him to join. She didn't succeed, he was too smart for that, but we can only guess at what methods of persuasion she used. Burns, like the hippies who came after him, enthusiastically subscribed to 'free love'. If he had not already, he most probably lost his virginity in Irvine.

Burns participation in 'free love' is purely speculative on my part - we have no record of how much or how little Burns' sex life profited by the influence of the Buchan cult. Carswell's book, appearing in the 1930's was deemed salacious and controversial, but Crawford (an academic from St Andrews University, writing in 2009) suggests that Burns was not overly promiscuous while in Irvine. One contributory factor being that he had a prolonged (three months) bout of illness. Crawford suggests that Burns was suffering from his first serious attack of depression. He called in the doctor but no reliable, convincing diagnosis was made of the condition (then or in his lifetime) that Burns called his 'hypochondria'. The word had a different meaning then and covered the symptoms we would today associate with depression, such as inexplicable aches and pains, nightmares, fevers, and general physical and mental fatigue. Some biographers suggest, with some justification, that Burns was a manic depressive. Others suggest that this first serious bout of illness in Irvine was a symptom of an underlying heart problem, caused by Burns' overwork and poor nutrition on his father's farm as a teenager.

After seven months of 'free love'/abstinence/depression – take your pick - Burns returned to Lochlea farm in 1782.

Lochlea was not doing well. William Burns was involved in costly litigation over his tenancy agreement and his health was fading. In November 1783 William moved the family to Mossgiel farm, near Mauchline.

On William's deathbed (he died 13 Feb 1784) he told Isabella, Burns' sister, that he had 'misgivings' about one of his children. Robert was present and asked if it was him, knowing full well it was, and his father's confirmation reduced him to tears.

Robert Burns loved and admired his father, despite their differences in temperament and wrote a moving epitath:

> O ye! who sympathise with Virtue's pains!
> Draw near with pious rev'rence & attend;
> Here lye the loving HUSBAND'S dear remains,
> The tender FATHER, and the generous FRIEND. –
>
> The pitying heart, that felt for human woe;
> The dauntless heart, that fear'd no human pride;
> The friend of man, to vice alone a foe;
> For 'even his failings lean'd to virtue's side.

Fatherhood (1784 to 1786)

The legal wrangle with the landlord over the tenancy agreement that had dogged William's last years and threatened to ruin the family financially had been settled just days before his death. So, Robert Burns became the head of the family. By all accounts he was devoted and conscientious in his new role.

However, in contrast to the sober, reliable head of the family, Robert was also developing an alter ego. He styled himself, in poems and letters, as Rob Mossgiel, a rakish fellow, a heavy drinker with an eye for the ladies. This other identity was fictional wish fulfillment, especially where drink was concerned.

Since his first serious episode of illness in Irvine, Burns found that his condition prevented him from drinking heavily and, although he didn't abstain, he drank in moderation thereafter. There are reports of him staying sober in otherwise very drunken company and very few reports of him ever drinking heavily. What rings truer is his avowed dedication to pursuing the opposite sex. He was very soon in relationships with various young women in Mauchline and, in 1784 and 1785, shared his affections between three: Elizabeth Paton, Elizabeth Miller and Jean Armour.

In 1784, Burns made Elizabeth Paton, a servant at Mossgiel farm, pregnant. He considered marrying her, but with the exception of his mother Agnes, his family didn't approve the match and he took their advice.

The Church held sway in moral matters and, in these days, pregnancy outside marriage was investigated and the sinners punished. The punishment for fornication was public humiliation. So it was that Robert Burns and Elizabeth Paton (probably in early 1785, when Elizabeth's pregnancy would be showing) were made
to sit on the 'cutty stool' in the nave at the front of the church in full view of the disapproving congregation. For additional humiliation they were clad in black sackcloth gowns of repentance.

This very public rebuke bred in Burns a distaste for the Church and his many romances following indicate a complete unwillingness or inability to see his actions as sinful.

In May 1785, Elizabeth Paton gave birth to Burns' first child, a daughter, also called Elizabeth. At some point she moved back to her family home, leaving the Burns family to care for the baby. Burns was a proud father, taking delight in the role, and writing an exuberant poem in Scottish dialect, using the 'Habbie stanza':

A Poet's Welcome to his Love Begotten Daughter (also titled, 'Welcome to a Bastart Wean')

[bastard; small one/baby]

Thou's welcome, wean; **mishanter fa' me**,　[bad luck to me]
If thoughts o' thee, or yet thy mamie,
Shall ever daunton me or awe me,
My bonie lady,
Or if I blush when thou shalt ca' me
Tyta or daddie.

Tho' now they ca' me fornicator,
An' tease my name in **kintry clatter**,　[country gossip]
The **mair** they talk, I'm **kent** the better,　[more, known]
E'en let them clash;
An auld wife's tongue's a feckless matter
To **gie ane fash**.　[to worry about]

Welcome! my bonie, sweet, wee **dochter**,　[daughter]
Tho' ye come here a wee unsought for,
And tho' your comin' I hae fought for,
Baith kirk and queir;　[both church and choir]
Yet, by my faith, ye're no unwrought for,
That I shall swear!

Wee image o' my bonie Betty,
As fatherly I kiss and **daut** thee,　[fondle]
As dear, and near my heart I set thee
Wi' as gude will
As a' the priests had seen me get thee
That's out o' hell.

Sweet fruit o' mony a merry **dint**,　[encounter]
My funny toil is now a' tint,
　　　　[my pleasant labour is not all wasted]
Sin' thou came to the warl' **asklent**,　[on the side]
Which fools may scoff at;
In my last plack thy part's be in't
The better ha'f o't.
　　　[you shall have the better half of my last farthing]
Tho' I should be the **waur bestead**, [the worse off for it]
Thou's be as braw and bienly clad,

> And thy young years as nicely bred
> Wi' education,
> As ony brat o' wedlock's bed,
> In a' thy station.
>
> Lord grant that thou may aye inherit
> Thy mither's person, grace, an' merit,
> An' thy poor, worthless daddy's spirit,
> Without his failins,
> 'Twill please me mair to see thee heir it,
> Than **stockit mailens**.   [well stocked farms]
>
> For if thou be what I wad **hae** thee,   [have]
> And tak the counsel I shall **gie** thee,   [give]
> I'll never rue my trouble wi' thee,
> The cost nor shame o't,
> But be a loving father to thee,
> And brag the name o't

At the same time as Burns, now aged 25, was dallying with Elizabeth Paton, he met nineteen year old Jean Armour. The story goes that their first meeting was when she chased Burns' dog away from dirtying her laundry as she was hanging it out to dry on a communal green. They met again at a local dance and she was soon under the spell of rakish Rob Mossgiel, and pregnant. They married, not in a public ceremony, but by a private agreement, which under Scots Law was legal and binding.

Sexual adventures aside, 1785 was a terrible year for Burns. At the end of the summer it became clear that his sixteen year old brother John was dying – eventually passing away in November. Also, Mossgiel farm was failing badly – when it came to farming, the Burns men seemed to have neither luck nor talent. So, facing financial ruin, and shouldering responsibility for the whole family (brothers, sisters and 'bastart weans') Burns began to dream of running off to Jamaica to be a plantation overseer.

Writing this in the oppressively 'woke' climate of 2020, I am aware that some people might immediately start crying, 'Slavery' and 'Cancel the Nazi Racist Burns'. Scotland is 'going broke for woke' at the moment: Edinburgh University has just removed the name David Hume (one of the world's greatest philosophers) from one of their buildings because of his alleged racism and association with slavery, while Glasgow and Edinburgh street names and statues are in danger of being changed or removed. At this level of madness, and if we don't all die of Covid 19, we will have to erase or rewrite the entire history of Britain, tear down all the statues, and set the wrecking balls loose on public buildings.

It strikes me as absurdly wrong to judge people of the past by today's standards, discount their achievements, and erase them from history if they fall short of the moveable feast of morality.

Slavery was widespread and practised as much by the indigenous races of Africa, Asia and the Middle East as white Europeans. Slavery was terrible but, let's face it, most of human history has been terrible: Genghis Khan had slaves; the Ancient Egyptians had slaves; the Ottoman Empire had slaves; the Ancient Greeks and the Ancient Romans had slaves. It didn't matter whether you were Christian or Islamic – both religions approved slaves. Britain was in the vanguard of stopping slavery and policed the world to ensure that the practice of slavery was abolished. For that Britain should be applauded not castigated.

The opening of L P Hartley's **The Go-Between** is very appropriate here: 'The past is a foreign country; they do things differently there.' Around thirty years ago, when you bought a book in a bookshop in the UK they placed it in a bag that had this quotation printed on it. This would be inconceivable today because 'wokeness' demands that we rewrite our history so that they do things in the past exactly the same as we do them today. Besides, Booksellers in 2020 would not dare use such a quotation, because even the word 'foreign' might cause offence.

I am not excusing Burns, but we have to understand him in the context of his life and times. At this point in his life, he was a failed farmer, and desperate to find a means of secure employment in a society of deep class prejudice and inequality. Burns, like the rest of us, was a product of his time and in all probability didn't give much thought to issues such as gender identity, slavery, or Vegan diets. Like your average German during Hitler's reign, Burns was faced with playing by the rules at the time or going under. If you think you are especially virtuous (and you may be - some exceptional people are) then look up the Zimbardo and Milgram experiments (especially the Stanford Prison one). Using experiments like these, psychologists have proven beyond any shadow of a doubt that very few of us possess the integrity and courage to stand up against prevailing systems, no matter how evil or unjust they may be. Burns was a sensitive, impoverished, poet farmer, not a political activist. Before the twentieth century, political activism was not tolerated – it was called sedition or treason, and the penalty was death.

At any rate, escape to Jamaica never became more than a fantasy, so perhaps Burns will be exempt from 'The Great Cancelling' - his books won't be burned and his statues won't be torn down.

Jean, Mary and Jamaica (1786)

In March 1786, Burns and Jean Armour went to her parents to announce that she was expecting his baby and that they had married, offering a document written by Burns as proof.

However, Burns found that his unsavoury reputation had preceded him and the furious parents refused to give their blessing. The Armours packed Jean off to a relative in Paisley and engaged a lawyer to annul the marriage. The lawyer performed some kind of mutilation of the document in order to appease the Armours, perhaps cutting the names out, but it is doubtful that would have overturned the legal force of Burns' agreement with Jean if the pair had stood their ground.

Burns was humiliated. He wrote, bitterly, about Jean in a letter to a friend. He took her obedience to her parents, her acceptance of exile to Paisley, as a terrible, unforgivable betrayal.

Before we feel too sorry for Burns, he wasted no time in finding a new object for his affection: Highland girl, Mary Campbell. Within days he had transferred his love to Mary (called Margaret in some accounts) and spent April and May with her, while pregnant Jean languished in disgrace in Paisley. As he had with Jean, Burns conducted a private marriage ceremony with

Mary (described in Catherine Carswell's **The Life of Robert Burns**, Chapter XVI April – May 1786; page 157). The ceremony, taking place by an unspecified stream or river, involved the gift of a two volume Bible which still exists and is held at the Brig o'Doon museum in Alloway.

Not much is known about the relationship between Burns and 'Highland Mary' – for reasons that will become clear in a few paragraphs - except that Burns intended to marry her formally and possibly planned to take her to Jamaica with him. She may also have been pregnant.

Following the meeting with the Armours and the imminent financial ruin of Mossgiel, Burns also had to contend with the fact that the Church were after him again for 'houghmagandie' (sex outside marriage) and he was facing another 'cutty stool' humiliation, only this time he would be in church with Jean and not Elizabeth Paton. In a letter in 1786 he wrote:

Already the holy beagles, the houghmagandie pack, begin to snuff the scent; & I expect every moment to see them cast off, & hear them after me in full cry: but as I am an old fox, I shall give them dodging & doubling for it; & by & bye, I intend to earth among the mountains of Jamaica.

(McIntyre, p.71)

It is no wonder that a confused and wounded Burns felt like a fox and indulged in a fantasy of escape to the ends of the earth. But, there was more at stake than money, or doing penance on the fornicator's stool in church. Burns must have worried about being found guilty of the serious charge of bigamy. With the marriage to Jean still not officially annulled, any investigation by the Church might uncover his hush-hush marriage to Mary Campbell. To protect himself he asked his priest to give him a 'bachelor's certificate'.

To further add to Burns' woes, he received a tip off that the Armours were about to issue a warrant threatening him with jail unless he provided financially for Jean's yet to be born baby. The net was closing but, to avoid the financial storm coming his way, Burns cannily signed over all his property to his brother Gilbert on 22nd July (and to his credit, made the proviso that Gilbert was to provide for Bess Paton, Burns' illegitimate daughter, until she reached 15 years of age).

Burns' 'bachelor's certificate' was granted in August 1786 after he completed his formal three church penances for fornication. The public dressing downs at Mauchline Kirk were less humiliating than his first time with Bess Paton. Because he and Jean were estranged, he was allowed to attend alone and sit in his own seat rather than suffer the added degradation of the 'cutty stool'.

Meanwhile, Mary Campbell had gone back to the Highlands to prepare for her new life with Robert, possibly in Jamaica. How long that plan lasted we don't know but it swiftly became a moot point, because Mary took ill. She died, probably of typhus, in October 1786. She had caught the disease from her sick brother, whom she was nursing at the time. Another possibility is that she was pregnant and died in childbirth. Whatever the truth, Burns was visibly devastated (observed by his sister) when he received the letter in November that told him of her passing and ever since viewed the affair with remorse, and never spoke of it. When he looked back at it years later he wrote some moving poetry about his 'Highland Mary'.

So 1785 and 1786 were turbulent, watershed years for Burns. The farm business had all but failed, he was in legal terms probably married to two women (for four or five months) and, with the Church 'houghmagandie pack' snapping at his heels, and the Armours issuing a writ for money or jail, Burns had reached his nadir. But fortune was about to swing in his favour. His Jamaica scheme was about to 'gang agley' in the best way possible.

Poems Chiefly in the Scottish Dialect was published 31 July 1786 in Kilmarnock. Robert Burns was 27 years old and on the brink of greatness.

Edinburgh (1786 to 1787)

The book was an instant success. It was praised by Dr Thomas Blacklock, highly respected in Edinburgh literary circles, who encouraged Burns to print a second edition. Jean Armour gave birth to twins (Robert and Jean) on 3rd September 1786 and Robert delighted in the fact that he was a father again. He set off for Edinburgh, on a borrowed pony, to plan for an Edinburgh edition of his poetry. He stayed in the capital for five months where he was lionised by high society, and the Freemasons of The Grand Lodge of Scotland toasted him as, 'Caledonia's Bard, Brother Burns'.

The unknown failure who wanted to escape to Jamaica at the beginning of the year had now become the most important literary figure in Scotland and a father again to boot.

Burns led a kind of double life in Edinburgh, mixing with high and low society. The flat he resided in, sharing a bed with his friend Richmond, was below a thriving brothel and, although I have never come across the suggestion that he used the services provided, Burns did gravitate towards some questionable characters, such as a young lawyer called Robert Ainslie. Ainslie is generally painted as something of a libertine by biographers, and the friendship lends weight to critics who emphasise the moral defects of Burns.

Burns was more drawn to the 'low life' than the 'high life' in Edinburgh and soon became disillusioned with his social 'superiors'. He realised that, in this class conscious city, he didn't quite fit in – he was a curiosity, he was the latest fad of the bored aristocracy. He wearied of his celebrity, realising that it was superficial, transitory and fragile. A brilliant speaker, he often made satirical comments during his orations at the dining tables of the rich and powerful, which were not always well received. My favourite was targeted at a church minister: 'Sir, I perceive that a man may be an excellent judge of poetry by square and rule and after all be a damned blockhead.' (Grimble, p. 65). A friend, Maria Riddell, revealed, 'For every ten jokes he got a hundred enemies.' (ibid.)

Four important events happened during his stay in 'the City of Sin' (as Edinburgh was viewed at the time by more parochial Scots).

The first was when Burns was introduced to a group called *The Crochallan Fencibles*, but we will save that until next chapter.

The second was when he visited the Canongate Churchyard and the unmarked grave of Robert Fergusson, the poet who had paved the way for his own use of the Scottish vernacular. Burns showed his admiration for Fergusson by commissioning a Headstone. The stonemason took two years to complete the work – so Burns deliberately delayed paying him for another two years!

The third was that Burns enjoyed another sexual relationship, this time with a young, servant girl called May (or in some accounts Margaret or Peggy) Cameron.

The fourth, was that the Edinburgh edition of **Poems Chiefly in the Scottish Dialect** was published in April 1787, selling 2,800 copies to subscribers. It was, roughly, a third bigger than the Kilmarnock edition. Burns sold the rights to the poems to his publisher Creech for a hundred guineas. What that actually meant for Burns' royalties or profits is unclear: McIntyre (p.139) points out that two thirds of the poems had already been printed in the Kilmarnock edition, and Burns had signed the rights for these over to his brother Gilbert the previous summer to stymie the writ from the Armours.

McIntyre estimates that £100 guineas in 1787 would be worth £30,000 in today's money. However, that may be a very modest estimate. It is difficult to find an average annual wage in 1787 but we know farm labourers were paid much less than £10 a year. The annual average salary in Britain today is over £25,000. If we make a very conservative estimate that £10 in 1780 equates to a low starting salary of £15,000 in 2020, then 100 guineas would have to be multiplied by 1,500 to give a modest estimate (a guinea was worth slightly more than a pound: £1 and a shilling, or £1.05 in decimal, but for ease of calculation let us assume guineas and pounds are the same).

So 100 guineas then would be worth around £150,000 in today's money – not the £30,000 that McIntyre suggests. Burns wrote that, after he paid printing costs, he had made about £400 clear.

He was probably understating the amount he made, but if we take him at his word then, in today's money, that equates to: 400 x 1,500 = £600,000.

Grimble (p.77) estimates that Burns actually earned £850 profit. Converting this to 2020 money we arrive at:

850 x 1500 = £1, 275,000 (over a million pounds!)

On top of this, further editions of the book were issued in London and America. It is possible that Burns became a very rich man indeed.

On the other hand, he worried about money – which is not to say that he had money worries. Most of us would be happy to have £600,000 to worry about!

Whatever he made from his poetry, Burns' money worries were soon to be over – through patronage (the connections he had made within the influential Edinburgh elite) he was soon to secure a job with the Excise as an Exciseman, a tax collector – a lucrative post that paid a basic wage three times higher than the average farm worker with generous bonuses for contraband seized.

Enjoying his new found money and fame, Burns set off from Edinburgh on a tour of the Borders with Robert Ainslie, in May 1787. He was not on a borrowed pony this time but on a newly purchased mare whom he named 'Jenny Geddes' after a feisty Presbyterian 'said to have flung a stool at a cleric' (Crawford, p.266) - Burns found it hard to resist making humorous barbs aimed at the establishment. The tour was the first of many he made, partly for publicity, partly for adventure, but mainly because he felt, as Scotland's Bard, he had to experience the whole country to truly live up to that appellation.

Still a single man, on the trip Burns had various flirtations which he reported in letters to friends.

Returning home in June, Burns received a begging letter written on behalf of May Cameron, the (probably illiterate) servant girl he had seduced in Edinburgh – she had, predictably, gotten pregnant and required financial assistance. Burns' letter in response is lost but his infamous letter about the matter to his friend Ainslie has survived. It does him no credit and gives ammunition to the argument put forward by Alan Cumming at the beginning of this book (that Burns treated women very badly):

> ... send for the wench and give her ten or twelve shillings, but don't for Heaven's sake meddle with her as a Piece...

Burns was home for two weeks during which time he met Jean again and made her pregnant before going off on another tour, of the Highlands this time, to enjoy his fame and wealth, and indulge his new passion - collecting Scottish songs.

Burns visited historic battle sites: Culloden and Bannockburn. He used a diamond stylus to engrave a poem on a window in a Stirling Inn, sympathising with the Jacobites and ridiculing the current Hanoverian line as 'An idiot race'. But, realising that this could get him in trouble, he returned to the Inn some weeks later and smashed the glass.

On this tour, Burns also met Neil Gow, the legendary Scottish fiddler who composed the wonderful 'Farewell to the whisky' and 'Welcome the whisky back again'. I used to think these were confessional titles suggesting Gow had tried sobriety for a while before joyously lapsing! Sadly, I was wrong - they refer to the government's 1799 ban on making whisky (something to do with a shortage of barley) and the lifting of the ban in 1801.

Back home Burns received a writ from May Cameron. It would seem, 'Ten or twelve shillings' wasn't enough child support - even in the 1780's. The writ was a proper legal document carrying with it the threat of jail. So, Burns dealt with it promptly, making some sort of final and complete settlement with her, the details of which have been lost in time. There is also no record of the child's birth or fate, and biographers have speculated that it was either stillborn, not Burns' child in the first place, or died soon after birth. Whatever the truth, May Cameron and her child played no further part in Burns' life.

At some point in 1787, when touring Scotland, Burns fell in love with Peggy Chalmers. He is reputed to have asked her to marry him, but was rejected.

In October 1787, Burns was back in Edinburgh, renting a room overlooking Saint Andrew's Square. Here the news reached him of the death of baby Jean, his daughter by Jean Armour. How the child died is not known but Burns took the news badly, and in a letter to his friend Richmond, hinted at 'carelessness', vaguely blaming the Armours. Burns went into a depression which he described, borrowing Fergusson's words, as 'bitter hours of blue devilism' (Crawford, p.278).

Nancy (1787 to 1788)

Burns' depression shifted when, at a tea party on 4th December, he met Mrs Agnes (Nancy) McLehose, daughter of a Glasgow surgeon, and was quickly besotted. She invited him to her house a few days later but, in the interim, Burns fell from a carriage onto the cobbled street and dislocated his knee. He was forced to decline the invitation. This early frustration characterised the rest of their relationship: passionate promise postponed.

In the absence of physical contact, their romance blossomed in a rapid and frequent exchange of letters, teasingly raising the stakes. Crawford (p. 280) explains that Edinburgh had a one hour postal delivery service at the time, so the romance between Burns and Nancy had something of the immediacy and flavour of an email romance today. In addition to the problem of Burns' temporary incapacity there was the small matter of 'Nancy' still being, technically, married. Although she was estranged from her abusive, lawyer husband – now overseeing a slave plantation in Jamaica – she feared for her good reputation in polite Edinburgh circles. To protect this, she and Burns adopted the pseudonyms: Clarinda (Nancy) and Sylvander (Burns).

Many letters survive and they make entertaining reading. It is unfair, cruel even, to mock the sensibilities of past generations but to the modern reader the letters verge on pastiche: there is much talk of virtue, piety, and souls. The elevated, formal English language of the Age of Reason is much in evidence (in distinct contrast to Burns' vernacular of the common man - Lowland Scots) and the pair engage in a 'higher' kind of love based on sexual abstinence. There is no doubt that the earthy, lusty Burns felt thwarted and would have preferred a more physical relationship, but Nancy was conventional for her gender, her times and her social class in morality and religious observance. Burns appeared to respect her intellect and, besides, had easy sexual outlets in servant girls and Jean, so was prepared to play the long game with Nancy. I think it is fair to say that both he and Nancy enjoyed the restraint, and both had the imagination and sensitivity to elevate it from sexually repressed titillation into a pure and perfect Platonic love. The pair did meet, before too long, in Nancy's quarters, for evenings of soul-bonding and passionate chastity. Burns tried his luck, but was unsuccessful in moving the relationship from the spiritual to carnal, except for one occasion which prompted a letter of repentance and restatement of the boundaries from Nancy:

> ...my heart reproaches me for last night... determine against everything but what the strictest delicacy warrants... Remember Clarinda's present and eternal happiness depends upon her adherence to Virtue...
> (McIntyre, p.201)

How far down the road of sinful carnality the couple travelled is unclear, but there is no suggestion that a full consummation took place. Apart from this blip, the relationship continued in chaste and lofty Virtue.

To give the flavour of this romance, here is an extract from a letter of Sylvander (Burns) to Clarinda (Nancy) (19 January 1788):

There is no time, my Clarinda, when the conscious thrilling chords of Love and Friendship give such delight, as in the pensive hours of what our favourite Thomson calls, 'Philosophic Melancholy.'

The sportive insects who bask in the sunshine of Prosperity, or the worms that luxuriant crawl amid their ample wealth of earth, they need no Clarinda; they would despise Sylvander- if they durst.

– The family of Misfortune, a numerous group of brothers and sisters! they need a resting-place to their souls: unnoticed, often condemned by the world; in some degree perhaps condemned by themselves, they feel the full enjoyment of ardent love, delicate tender endearments, mutual esteem and mutual reliance.-

In this light I have often admired Religion.-In proportion as we are wrung with grief, or distracted with anxiety, the ideas of a compassionate Deity, an Almighty Protector, are doubly dear.-
' 'Tis this, my friend, that streaks our morning bright;
' 'Tis this that gilds the horrors of our night'

I have been this morning taking a peep thro', as Young finely says, 'the dark postern of time long elaps'd;' and you will easily guess, 'twas a rueful prospect.-What a tissue of thoughtlessness, weakness and folly!

My life reminded me of a ruin'd temple: what strength, what proportion in some parts! what unsightly gaps, what prostrate ruins III others! I kneele down before the Father of mercies and said, 'Father, I have sinned against Heaven and in thy sight, and am no more worthy to be called thy son!' I rose, eased and strengthened.-I despise the superstition of a Fanatic, but I love the Religion of a Man. – 'The future,' said I to myself, 'is still before me: there let me-

On Reason build Resolve,
'That column of true majesty in Man!'

'I have difficulties many to encounter,' said I: 'but they are not 'absolutely insuperable: and where is firmness of mind shewn, but 'in exertion? mere declamation, is bombast rant.- Besides, wherever I am, or in whatever situation I may be-

-' 'Tis nought to me:
'Since God is ever present, ever felt, 'In the void waste as in the city full;
'And where He vital breathes, there must be joy!'

Saturday Night-half after ten

What luxury of bliss I was enjoying this time yesternight! My everdearest Clarinda, you have stolen away my soul but you have refined, you have exalted it; you have given it a stronger sense of Virtue, and a stronger relish for Piety. -Clarinda, first of your Sex, if ever I am the veriest wretch on earth to forget you; if ever your lovely image is effaced from my soul,

'May I be lost, no eye to weep my end;
'And find no earth that's base enough to bury me!
…

The letter continues in similar vein. If you are a glutton for punishment, you can read the full version here:
https://burnsletters.wordpress.com/category/clarinda/
(or buy the book: the letters have been published).

Burns signs off:

Goodnight, my dear Clarinda!

Sylvander

While Burns pursued the purest Platonic love with Nancy he was less devout with her servant, Jenny Clow, a twenty year old Fife girl. Nancy had sent her to Burns with a message and he, apparently seeing no contradiction in his actions, seduced her. Jenny was to give birth to his son in November 1788.

The relationship between Burns and Nancy was a case of delayed gratification, at first delightful and delicious, but eventually souring. Reading between the lines (of the letters) I believe that Nancy, despite her religious and moral objections, wanted Burns to seduce her. But Burns, although free and easy with girls below his social and intellectual station, appeared to have difficulty seducing upper class ladies. Why, we can only speculate. Perhaps he had no modus operandi: his 'training' in rural Ayrshire, particularly in Irvine, had not equipped him to deal with intelligent, upper class women. Perhaps he had an inferiority complex that rendered him psychologically incapable of risking rejection from a lady he grudgingly deferred to. At any rate class became an insurmountable barrier, probably both socially and psychologically.

Meanwhile, Jean was pregnant again and her enraged parents were about to throw her out on the streets. Burns, hearing this, asked friends to shelter her while he was in Edinburgh.

When Burns returned to Mauchline in February 1788 he promised to look after Jean, and square matters with her parents, under the proviso that 'neither during his life nor after his death' would she attempt any claim on him as a husband, even though any one should persuade her that she had such a claim, which she had not.' (Carswell, p.263). Jean agreed. He did indeed reach peace with the Armours – his newfound fame and wealth possibly smoothing the way.

Burns' attitude to Jean was appalling. There is no justification for it in today's morality, but we must remember that this was a time when women were very much second class citizens, regarded as inferior and subservient to men. Burns was the product of a society of deep, institutionalised misogyny so his baseline attitude is shocking and, perhaps, incomprehensible, to the modern reader. Further, Burns clearly harboured great resentment against Jean for acceding to her parents' wishes and abandoning him. Despite this, he still thought of her, cared for her and desired her. Somehow he had to reconcile these feelings with his unwillingness to commit to her. He was happy to make love to Jean, and have children with her, but made it clear that he would never marry her and that she would have no claim on him. That she accepted these terms reflects badly on both of them.

In romantic matters, Burns had the capacity to love more than one woman at a time. Sometimes he was caring Robert Burns and other times he was ruthless, rakish Rob Mossgiel. To put it kindly, he could compartmentalise his emotions. To put it less kindly, whether through self-deception, or manic depressive insensitivity, or misogyny, he was capable of outrageous duplicity.

Jean gave birth to twin girls on 13th March, 1788, while Burns was back in Edinburgh. One child died on 10th March, and the other on 22nd March.

Perhaps it was this misfortune that jolted Burns back to reality, because he came to the realisation that his fantasy relationship with Nancy was leading nowhere and that he needed the security of family and farm. It was time to settle down and Burns realised that a refined (and still married) Edinburgh lady wouldn't be much good as a farmer's wife. Jean, with whom he already enjoyed a gratifying physical relationship, was a much more pragmatic choice.

So, Burns abandoned his Edinburgh life and decided to use his newfound wealth to reinvent himself as a 'gentleman farmer'. He took on the lease of scenic Ellisland farm near Dumfries. Also, still worried about money, he pulled strings with his newfound upper class connections and was offered a well-paid position with the Excise, which he was to begin in the late summer of 1788. He was going to be a happily married man and secure his family's fortunes by combining farming with a steady job.

The new direction worked well and Burns found domestic happiness. Jean adored him and he wrote to a friend, Mrs Dunlop, that he believed in Jean he had, 'got the handsomest figure, the sweetest temper, the soundest constitution, and the kindest heart in the country.' (McIntyre p. 236). In a letter sent in April he said he had married Jean (another private arrangement) and reaffirmed this in a letter to Ainsley on the 26th May. The marriage of Jean Armour and Robert Burns was officially registered in the Mauchline parish records on 5th August 1788. Perhaps rakish Rob Mossgiel was settling down?

For her part, Nancy must have eventually had to square her idealised love for Burns with the fact that he had not only impregnated her servant, but was now also committed to Jean.

We will leave Burns at this point, May in 1788, as he makes preparations to settle down with Jean as Exciseman, gentleman farmer, poet and songsmith. Let us look at one of his most famous songs. He referred to it, modestly, as a 'simple old Scots song which I had picked up in the country' but it is almost certainly his own work, mostly if not entirely. This is the song named by American singer-songwriter Bob Dylan as having had the biggest impact on him: Burns' 1794 song 'A Red, Red Rose' also known as, 'My Luve is like a Red, Red, Rose'.

Nature: the Imagery of Love

My Luve is Like a Red, Red Rose

Original	Modern Translation
O my Luve's like a red, red rose That's newly sprung in june; O my Luve's like the melodie That's sweetly play'd in tune:	O my Love is like a red, red rose That's newly sprung in June; O my Love is like the melody That's sweetly played in tune:
As fair art thou, my bonnie lass, So deep in luve am I: And I will luve thee still, my dear, Till a' the seas gang dry:	As fair are you, my lovely girl, So deep in love am I: And I will love you still, my dear, Till all the seas go dry:
Till a' the seas gang dry, my dear, And the rocks melt wi' the sun: I will luve thee still, my dear, While the sands o' life shall run.	Till all the seas go dry, my dear, And the rocks melt with the sun: I will love you still, my dear, While the sands of life shall run.
And fare thee weel, my only Luve And fare thee weel, a while! And I will come again, my Luve, Tho' it were ten thousand mile.	And fare you well, my only Love And fare you well, a while! And I will come again, my Love, Though it were ten thousand miles.

Commentary

In the first verse Burns captures the joy of being in love. The rose is an early and enduring symbol of beauty. The repetition and alliteration of 'red, red rose' gives emphasis to the power of its colour and the second line about it being 'newly sprung' echoes the light, fresh feeling of new love. Red symbolises passion and June is the beginning of summer. The final two lines compare his love to a melody played in tune. These ideas (love being associated with roses, summer and music) are common tropes in poetry, but have never before or since been so simply and perfectly expressed.

The next verse is plain speaking, devoid of metaphor, a simple statement that he will love her until all the seas run dry. This acknowledgement that Time will end introduces the idea (again, one that has been expressed many times before and since) that we are mortal, linked to nature and temporality.

In the third verse, the speaker expands upon the temporal theme, repeating the image of the seas going dry and adding the idea of rocks melting in the sun to describe the end of planet Earth. This was a relatively new theory then and Colin Will makes an interesting point:

Geology as a science was brand new at the time Burns was writing; this is a very modern poem. And where was his inspiration? I submit that he got these ideas either directly from James Hutton, the Berwickshire farmer sometimes called the 'Father of Modern Geology', or from Hutton's friend Sir James Hall of Dunglass. The two men in a boat discovered the famous unconformity at Siccar Point, near where I live, where an ocean going dry formed a sandstone which was eroded and folded upright, then overlain after an unimaginable interval by another ocean, which also ran dry.

Hutton and Hall were among the distinguished men and women of Edinburgh society we know Burns met during his time in the city.

https://www.scottishpoetrylibrary.org.uk/poem/red-red-rose/

The 'sands of life' image of the final line may well have been inspired by the Geological discoveries of his time but it also echoes Genesis 22:17:

'I will surely bless you, and I will surely multiply your offspring as the stars of heaven and as the sand that is on the seashore.'

This metaphor therefore links not only life itself but Burns' love to eternity. His love is both physical and spiritual.
    The final verse is a parting, with the speaker promising to meet his love again, though it 'be ten thousand mile'.

In this next love song Burns once again draws on Nature for his imagery. The Romantic association of Nature with innocence and intense feelings is present, if not quite elevated to a mystical experience.

Ye Banks and Braes o' Bonnie Doon

Original	Modern Translation
Ye banks and braes o' bonnie Doon, How can ye bloom sae fresh and fair; How can ye chant, ye little birds, And I sae weary, fu' o' care! Thou'lt break my heart, thou warbling bird, That wantons thro' the flowering thorn: Thou minds me o' departed joys, Departed—never to return!	You river banks and hills of lovely Doon, How can you bloom so fresh and fair; How can you sing, you little birds, When I'm so weary, full of care! You'll break my heart, you warbling bird, Moving carefree through the flowering thorn: You remind me of long-lost joys, Departed—never to return!
Aft hae I rov'd by bonnie Doon, To see the rose and woodbine twine; And ilka bird sang o' its luve, And fondly sae did I o' mine. Wi' lightsome heart I pu'd a rose, Fu' sweet upon its thorny tree; And my fause luver stole my rose, But, ah! he left the thorn wi' me.	I've often wandered by lovely Doon, To see the rose and woodbine twine; And every bird sang of its love, And fondly, so did I of mine. With light heart I pulled a rose, So sweet upon its thorny tree; And my false lover stole my rose, But, ah! he left the thorn in me.

Glossary
Doon – the Doon river
Braes – steep banks or hillside
Wanton = careless or, in this context, carefree
Ilka = every
Fause = false

Commentary

In this lyric the speaker is a young woman, deeply in love, observing nature and how a bird moves carefree through the 'flowering thorn'. This is symbolic of how she once lived, innocent and unaware of the dangers ('thorns') of life but now she is 'weary' and 'full of care'.

In the second verse we find out why. A false lover 'stole my rose' and 'left the thorn wi' me'. Burns uses the symbol of love, the rose, in a very different way from 'My Luve is Like a Red, Red Rose'. Here it suggests multiple meanings. Once interpretation is that the false lover has taken advantage of her love and innocence, leaving her bitter ('he left the thorn wi' me') but another possibility is that the rose is symbolic of her virginity. This metaphor suggests the false lover has taken what used to be referred to as her 'maidenhood' and left her pregnant. The child is the 'thorn' and will be a painful reminder of the fact that she has been betrayed.

The song was inspired by a true story involving a woman Burns met when she was 18. Margaret (Peggy) Kennedy (1766-1795) had been seduced and abandoned by Andrew McDougall, son of a wealthy family and a Member of Parliament. Margaret died before the court case concluded but McDougall was ordered to pay into her estate and provide for the child.

Ae Fond Kiss

The final song in this chapter is, in my opinion, the most beautiful love song ever written.

A key feature of Romanticism was an excess of emotion and in this lyric Burns lays bare his heart. If you had difficulty understanding my explanation of The Sublime is (in Chapter 2) then, listening to Eddi Reader singing this song should make it clear – I challenge anyone to listen to it without being reduced – no, uplifted - to a weeping, sobbing, blubbering wreck.

The song was inspired by Burns' unconsummated love affair with 'Nancy' McLehose. A brief recap: they met during his stay in Edinburgh after his book had been published and he was embraced by Edinburgh society and at the height of his fame. They exchanged passionate love letters using the pseudonyms Clarinda and Sylvander and spent many evenings in each others' company. Burns, even when married to Jean in August 1788, kept up a correspondence with Nancy, and continued to have deep feelings for her. When he heard that she was leaving Edinburgh to travel to Jamaica in December 1791, to be reunited with her husband, he wrote 'Ae Fond Kiss', and sent it to her before she departed. They never met again, although forty years later Nancy/Clarinda/Agnes McLehose, at the age of 72, wrote:

This day I never can forget. Parted with Burns, in the year 1791, never more to meet in this world, Oh may we meet in Heaven.
(6th December 1831)

Ae Fond Kiss

Original	Modern Translation
Ae fond kiss, and then we sever; Ae fareweel, alas, for ever! Deep in heart-wrung tears I'll pledge thee, Warring sighs and groans I'll wage thee!	One affectionate kiss and then we part; A goodbye, sadly, forever! Deep in heart-wrung tears I'll pledge you, Warring sighs and groans I'll wage you!
Who shall say that Fortune grieves him While the star of hope she leaves him? Me, nae cheerfu' twinkle lights me, Dark despair around benights me.	Who shall say that Fortune grieves him While the star of hope she leaves him? Me, no cheerful twinkle lights me, Dark despair around benights me.
I'll ne'er blame my partial fancy; Naething could resist my Nancy; But to see her was to love her, Love but her, and love for ever.	I'll never blame my partial fancy; Nothing could resist my Nancy; But to see her was to love her, Love but her, and love for ever.
Had we never loved sae kindly, Had we never loved sae blindly, Never met—or never parted, We had ne'er been broken-hearted.	Had we never loved so kindly, Had we never loved so blindly, Never met—or never parted, We had never been broken-hearted.
Fare thee weel, thou first and fairest! Fare thee weel, thou best and dearest!	Fare you well, you first and fairest! Fare you well, you best and dearest!

Thine be ilka joy and treasure, Peace, enjoyment, love, and pleasure!	Yours be every joy and treasure, Peace, enjoyment, love, and pleasure!
Ae fond kiss, and then we sever! Ae fareweel, alas, for ever! Deep in heart-wrung tears I'll pledge thee, Warring sighs and groans I'll wage thee!	One affectionate kiss and then we part A goodbye, sadly, forever! Deep in heart-wrung tears I'll pledge you, Warring sighs and groans I'll wage you!

Glossary
Ae (pronounced 'Ay' as in 'pay') = one
Sever = separate, part
Wage = pledge or bet
Sae = so
fare thee weel = farewell
ilka = every

Commentary

The speaker is addressing a loved one, Nancy, and expressing the heartache he feels at losing her forever.

In the very first line, Burns' choice of 'sever' captures the pain he is feeling: this isn't just a parting, it is a cutting off, an amputation. It suggests that he and 'Nancy' are joined and must be cut apart; it implies something irrevocable, painful, and final.

Powerful emotions continue to be expressed – his tears are 'heart wrung': they are being squeezed or pressured out of him. 'Warring sighs and groans' expresses his inner turmoil; he is sighing with despair, and groaning with pain. The first stanza ends with the imagery of having lost hope and being plunged into darkness and despair.

In stanza two he praises his love, and makes the point that if they had never loved so 'kindly' and 'blindly', and had never met, then they would not be in such pain ('so broken-hearted').

In the final stanza, he bids her farewell, wishing her every 'joy and treasure', followed by a restatement of the pain he is feeling.

Chapter 5

Nature: Celebrating the Bawdy Body

Green Grow the Rashes O
Comin' Thro' the Rye

'Let them cant about decorum,
who have characters to lose!'

WARNING: You should really skip past this chapter if you are a respectable member of society, regular churchgoer, under the age of 18, or of a prudish disposition.

Now we look at Burns in a lighter, more humorous vein as he celebrates- one of our most powerful, natural urges, the urge to procreate.

'Bawdy' is coarse or vulgar humour; often to do with bodily functions, especially sex, and Burns revelled in it. As you may have gathered by now, he was a very naughty man.

In my childhood in 'the Swinging Sixties' Scotland was still religiously conservative and prudish about sexual matters. This attitude was partly a throwback to the Victorian age but also deeply rooted in Scottish Calvinism.

Not being a theologian I can only give a layman's impression of Calvinism. It seems to me that it was (is) a particularly miserable branch of Protestantism that saw humanity as essentially sinful. A central belief was that very few of us would get to Heaven (and it was 'preoradained': i.e. God had already decided who the chosen few were - what a curious notion!) and that the majority of us were irredeemable sinners bound for hell and damnation.

The combination of Calvinism and the abysmal Scottish weather is almost certainly the source of the stereotype of 'the dour Scot'. The popular BBC television comedy **Dad's Army** (about the British Home Guard in World War 2 – in case you are unfamiliar with the show) featured a stereotypical Scottish character called Private Frazer, a coffin maker by trade, whose catchphrase was, 'We're all doomed!' Yes, cheery old Calvinism.

The most influential religious figure in Scottish Calvinism was (and still is) John Knox (C. 1514 – 1572). Knox's brand of hellfire and damnation Calvinism influenced the Puritans who abandoned sinful England to set up a new Eden in America. They were another jolly bunch – not keen on dancing or theatre, but always cock-a-hoop for a good witch trial.

Knox was also big on misogyny, and wrote an essay with what has to be my favourite title ever: 'The First Blast of the TRUMPET Against the MONSTRUOUS Regiment of Women' (1558). In this gem, he attacks female monarchs, arguing that having female rulers is against the teachings of **The Bible**. He found himself at odds several times with Mary Queen of Scots and narrowly avoided being accused of treason.

https://en.wikipedia.org/wiki/The_First_Blast_of_the_Trumpet_Against_the_Monstruous_Regiment_of_Women

Calvinism impacted directly on Burns. In Scotland, to have sex outside marriage was sinful and public shaming was commonplace. Everyone attended church and at the front of the church nave was a 'cutty stool' (or 'cuttie stoole') where known fornicators were forced to sit during the church service, in full view of the congregation. As mentioned last chapter, Burns had to endure this humiliation in 1784 at the age of 25 with the family servant, Elizabeth Paton.

Burns was unabashed and wrote a bawdy verse to commemorate the occasion. Here is an excerpt:

ROBt BURNS The Fornicator

...

Before the Congregation wide,
I passed the muster fairly,   (presented myself well?)
My handsome Betsy by my side,
We gat oor ditty rarely;   (ditty = indictment, charge)
But my downcast ee did chance to spy   (ee = eye)
What made my lips to watter,
 Thae limbs sae clean where I between
Commenced a Fornicator.

...

So, even as he is being told off in church, Burns is admiring the legs of his lover, and salivating as he lusts after her!

Burns wrote a fair amount of bawdy verse, not intended for publication, and circulated it (often in letters) among his more broadminded friends. He found a public forum for his bawd when he was invited to join **The Crochallan Fencibles** in Edinburgh. These kinds of gentlemen's clubs were common at the time and often had mock military titles or the kind of names we might give our Pub Quiz Teams today. The **Fencibles** would meet in an Edinburgh pub (in Anchor Close off the High Street to be precise) to drink, talk and get up to all sorts of merry japes and laddish mischief. Burns delighted in entertaining them with lewd verse.

After his death Burns bawdy offerings (including the one above) were collected and published under the title, **The Merry Muses of Caledonia**. You can either purchase it or find a free pdf online. But be warned – it is filthy – lots of the F word and the C word, liberal doses of sex, and some farting. Here are two more choice excerpts:

Burns on the evergreen subject of genital topiary:

Nae Hair On't

Yestreen I wed a lady fair,
An ye wad believe me,

On her cunt there growes nae hair,
That's the thing that grieves me.

It vexed me sair, it plagued me sair,
It put me in a passion,
To think that I haed wad a wife,
Whase cunt was oot o fashion.

Burns was writing in the tradition of Scottish bawd, which loved to use 'the C word' and was fixated on pubic hair for some reason. Here is a final disgusting example, a verse from a filthy version of 'Green Grow the Rashes O':

O wat ye ocht & fisher Meg,
An how she **trowed** the wabster, O,   [rolled = had sex with; the weaver]
She loot me see her carrot cunt,   [let]
An sell'd it for a labster, O.   [sold it for a lobster]

Clearly Burns could not have published these obscenities in his lifetime without serious disapproval, not least from the Church. He did, however, for public consumption, write a few songs that patrolled the borders of taste without crossing them.

Here are two such songs:

Nature: Celebrating the Bawdy Body

Green Grow the Rashes O

Original	Modern Translation
CHORUS. Green grow the rashes, O! Green grow the rashes, O! The sweetest hours that e'er I spend Are spent amang the lasses, O. There's nought but care on ev'ry han', In every hour that passes, O: What signifies the life o' man, An' 'twere na for the lasses, O. The warly race may riches chase, An' riches still may fly them, O; An' tho' at last they catch them fast, Their hearts can ne'er enjoy them, O. But gie me a canny hour at e'en, My arms about my dearie, O; An' warly cares, an' warly men, May a' gae tapsalteerie, O.	CHORUS. Green grow the rashes, O! Green grow the rashes, O! The sweetest hours that ever I spend Are spent among the girls (or women), O. There's nothing but care on every hand, In every hour that passes, O: What signifies the life of man, If it were not for the women, O. The worldly race may riches chase, And riches still may fly them, O; And though at last they catch them fast, Their hearts can never enjoy them, O. But give me a quiet hour in the evening, My arms about my loved one, O; And worldly cares, and worldly men, May all go topsy-turvy, O.

For you sae douce, ye sneer at this, Ye're nought but senseless asses, O: The wisest man the warl' e'er saw, He dearly lov'd the lasses, O.	For you so respectable, you sneer at this, You're nothing but senseless asses, O: The wisest man the world every saw, He dearly loved the women, O.
Auld Nature swears the lovely dears Her noblest work she classes, O: Her 'prentice han' she try'd on man, An' then she made the lasses, O.	Old Nature swears the lovely dears Her noblest work she classes, O: Her apprentice hand she tried on man, And then she made the women, O.
Green grow the rashes, O! Green grow the rashes, O! The sweetest hours that e'er I spend Are spent amang the lasses, O.	Green grow the rashes, O! Green grow the rashes, O! The sweetest hours that ever I spend Are spent among the women, O.

Glossary
war'ly-worldly
cannie-quiet
tapsalteerie-topsy-turvy
douce-respectable

Nature: Celebrating the Bawdy Body

Commentary

This song, published in 1784, makes more sense if we consider the attitudes to sex at the time. I see 'Green Grow the Rashes O' as Burns' reaction to the Calvinist prohibition on 'fornication'. The 'rashes' are bulrushes (long green leaf-like plants) that grow at the edge of lakes and rivers. Burns is using them as a metaphor for the fecundity of Nature and, in the chorus, comparing his love of the lasses with them, as something natural and positive. He claims his 'sweetest hours' are spent with females.

The first stanza suggests that our lives are basically defined ('signified') as hour after hour of worry ('nought but care on ev'ry han'). The last line counters that, suggesting that if it was not for women that is all our lives would mean.

The second stanza, describes the empty pursuit of money. We never seem to get rich, and even if we did we wouldn't enjoy our 'riches' anyway.

In stanza three Burns tells us that all he needs is a quiet hour with his lover for all his worldly cares to disappear in a chaotic whirl.

In stanza four he takes a poke at the 'douce' (respectable), calling them 'senseless assess'. Burns saw promiscuity as more natural and wise than conforming to the repressive ways of society.

The final stanza is a beautiful idea and gets Burns big credit with feminists. Burns suggests that Nature's first, apprentice attempt at making life (her 'prentice han') was to make Man but then she used her tried and tested skills to make Woman. Therefore, a feminist would conclude, he is saying that women are superior to men. And he sort of is! But we might equally validly conclude that this is Burns expressing his deep admiration for women as a confirmed, promiscuous romantic.

Burns wrote this about his lyric:

I do not see that the turn of mind and pursuits of such a one as the following verses describe - who swoons thro' the vale of life, amusing himself with every little flower that fortune throws in his way, is, in the least, more inimical to the sacred interests of piety and virtue. I do not see but he may gain heaven as well as he who, straining straight forward, and perhaps bespattering all about him, gains some of life's little eminences, where, after all, he can only see and be seen a little more conspicuously than he whom in the pride of his heart, he is apt to term the poor, indolent devil he has left behind him.

This is a clever piece of writing. In Catherine Carswell's **Robert Burns**, (p.72) she details how, as a teenager, he delighted in debating and could argue any topic from either side. His skill was legendary and he bested his Maths teacher in such a debate.

This short passage is a good example of Burns' discursive talent. It is also pure Romanticism.

Let's look at the ideas contained.

Firstly, Burns writes of one who 'swoons through the vale of life' – to swoon is to faint or fall into a state of rapture – in other words to be overcome by an excess of emotion – a very Romantic notion of experiencing the Sublime in Nature. So, he is saying that the lover is, in a sense, virtuous and promiscuity is therefore acceptable, holy even.

Secondly, 'vale' is short for valley and reminds us of the Biblical phrase: 'though I walk through the valley of the shadow of death' (King James Bible, Psalm 23:4). Burns alludes to this phrase in order to argue that the swooning lover, sampling the delights of 'every little flower' (every woman) is just as holy as the religious man, who conforms to society for personal gain ('eminences' suggests status or privileges; and 'pride' is one of the seven deadly sins).

Burns describes the religious man as 'straining straight forward', implying that his behaviour is unnatural, an effort made in order to climb the social ladder so that he can look down on others and feel superior. Further, the religious man is 'perhaps bespattering all about him' suggesting that his pious behaviour contaminates and causes harm to others.

In this short polemic are all the ingredients of Romanticism: linking Nature to the divine, celebrating emotional excess, and challenging the social and moral values of the day.

'Green Grow the Rashes O' appeared in the Scots Musical Museum (1787) and is a celebration of love using the imagery of the natural world to declare both Burns admiration for women and his appreciation of the power of Nature. It is a song of Life over anti-life, Calvinist doctrine.

As a footnote: about seven years ago I attended a concert by traditional Scottish musicians Phil Cunningham and Ally Bain, where Phil made a joke about the Mexican insult 'gringo' (reserved for foreigners, especially white people) deriving from this song ('Green grow' sounds like 'gringo').

I took this theory with a pinch of salt until researching for this book and found a few online sources, including Wikipedia, which give it credence. Apparently, during the Mexican War (1846 to 1848) American soldiers sang Burns' song and another one called, 'Green Grows the Laurel' and this led to locals referring to the Yankees as 'gringos'.

It could be nonsense, but I like to think it is true.

Comin' Thro' the Rye

Original	Modern Translation
O, Jenny's a' weet, poor body, Jenny's seldom dry; She **draigl't** a' her petticoattie, Comin thro' the rye!	Oh, Jenny's all **wet**, poor thing, Jenny's seldom dry; She's dragging all her petticoats Coming through the rye.
Comin thro' the rye, poor body, Comin thro' the rye, She **draigl't** a' her petticoattie, Comin thro' the rye!	Coming through the rye, poor thing, Coming through the rye. She's **dragging** all her petticoats Coming through the rye.

Gin a body meet a body Comin thro' the rye Gin a body kiss a body, Need a body cry?	**Given** that a person meets a person Coming through the rye, If a person kisses a person, Need anybody cry?
Comin thro' the rye, poor body, Comin thro the rye, She **draigl't** a' her petticoattie, Comin thro' the rye!	Coming through the rye, poor thing, Coming through the rye. She's dragging all her petticoats Coming through the rye.
Gin a body meet a body Comin thro' the glen, Gin a body kiss a body, Need the warld ken?	Should somebody meet somebody Coming through the glen, Should somebody kiss somebody, Need all the **world know**?
Comin thro' the rye, poor body, Comin thro' the rye, She draigl't a' her petticoattie, Comin thro' the rye!	Coming through the rye, poor thing, Coming through the rye. She's dragging all her petticoats Coming through the rye.
Gin a body meet a body Comin thro' the grain; Gin a body kiss a body, The thing's a body's ain.	Should somebody meet somebody Coming through the grain, Should somebody kiss somebody, The thing's somebody's **own** (business).

Glossary
weet – wet
draigl't – draggled, dragging something until it gets wet and muddy
gin – given, in the sense of 'if'
cry – could mean to call out [for help], but, given Burns' celebration of sex and rejection of the repressive views of the church, most likely means that this is a private moment of passion between two lovers which is to be relished and is no business of anybody else.
warl – world
ken – know
ain – own

Commentary

The first question we might ask is: what does 'Coming through the rye' mean?

It could be that Jenny, the girl in the song, is walking through fields of rye (a grain related to barley and wheat, used for flour, bread, and whisky, among other things). However, Burns was borrowing from an older Scottish song which referred to the Rye river, and 'Comin' thro' the rye' was a North Ayrshire phrase for crossing the Rye river at a ford. No one really knows and it doesn't matter as the song is really about sex and both interpretations (river and crop) work equally well here as metaphors for fecundity.

The poem is a celebration of sexual passion and exists in many different versions. Burns took a bawdy original and sanitised it for publication in **The Scots Musical Museum**).

In first verse, Burns shows sympathy for Jenny, calling her 'poor'. There is also a titillating reference (titillating in the 18th century at least) to her petticoat (a frilly, skirt-like undergarment) and the fact that it is 'wet' and that Jenny is 'seldom dry'.

The images in the lyric are more than hinting at a sexual encounter, and in the bawdy original, the lovers do more than 'kiss'.

In the third verse Burns asks if the world needs to know about the meeting, and states in the final line of the fourth verse that, 'The thing's a body's ain' – in other words, it's the lovers' own business and no concern of anyone else's. Burns is showing sympathy for Jenny, who is just doing what comes naturally and should not be judged harshly by the repressive society of the time.

PART THREE

POLITICS

Chapter 6

The Politics of Rebellion: Burns, Wallace and the Jacobites

'Scots Wha Hae'
'Charlie, He's my Darling'
'Ye Jacobites by Name'

'Man's inhumanity to man
makes countless thousands mourn!'

Before we return to Burns' life we are going to spend this and the next chapter looking at the history and political ideas that shaped Burns' times and his thought.

We will begin our journey in 1314 with a consideration of the dysfunctional relationship between Scotland and England, the abusive relationship between Catholics and Protestants, and the festering acrimony between Monarchists and Republicans (which was even worse than the current enmity between Democrats and Republicans, although the USA appears to be catching up!). We will also throw in a little Shakespeare, some fireworks, and an idea that used to be all the rage, but has now become rather unfashionable, 'the Divine Right of Kings'.

Scots Wha Hae

When Burns was a child he had two favourite books: **The Life of Hannibal** and **The History of Sir William Wallace**. Of the latter he wrote, 'the story of Wallace poured a Scottish prejudice into my veins which will boil along there till the flood-gates of life shut in eternal rest.' (Grimble, p. 20)

Burns visited the ancient battlefield of Bannockburn in 1787 and wrote the stirring battle cry that is 'Scots Wha Hae' in 1793.

In 1314 Scotland was (to simplify a complex situation) under the control of England. William Wallace had briefly ruled Scotland before King Edward I of England took control back, capturing and executing Wallace in 1305. Scots and English have been squabbling ever since.

The execution scene in the film **Braveheart** (1995), starring Mel Gibson as William Wallace, was gruesome but even that was sanitised when compared to the real thing.

Wallace's execution started after he had been found guilty of treason at Westminster. He was dragged naked through the London streets by horses, for six miles, while the English crowds whipped him, beat him with sticks, and pelted him with excrement and garbage. Next, when he arrived at Smithfield, the Executioner tortured him for a long, long time, in front of a highly entertained audience, cutting off his genitals and then removing his intestines – all the while keeping him alive. Eventually, Wallace was beheaded and 'quartered' (his body torn into four pieces by having four horses pull in different directions). His remains were then distributed throughout the kingdom and displayed publically to deter further acts of insurrection.

Robert the Bruce was a Scottish nobleman who decided to take up Wallace's cause. I have always wondered why he was called 'the Bruce'. His name was Robert de Brus (as he was part descended from the Normans who invaded Britain in 1066) – which meant 'of Brus' (a place in Normandy, France). So, in Scottish, this became Robert of Bruce and then, Robert the Bruce.

The Bruce was crowned King of Scotland in March 1306, much to the annoyance of the English King Edward I, who promptly dispatched an army to squash him. Bruce was defeated in June 1306 at the Battle of Methven and forced into hiding. Over the years that followed, Robert the Bruce waged guerrilla warfare until he had raised enough support to secure various areas of Scotland under his rule.

However, the day of reckoning was coming.

Edward II (who had succeeded to the throne in 1307) sent a mighty English army north in 1314 with the intention to 'shock and awe', decimate, pulverise, and annihilate.

Bruce knew that to gain independence for Scotland he would have to defeat this larger and superior force, which not only outnumbered the Scots two to one, but were regarded as the finest army in the medieval world.

It was all looking rather hopeless for Scotland.

By now, though, Robert the Bruce was a seasoned campaigner, and a clever strategist. He knew that Bannockburn, near Stirling, was a key strategic point. It was, and still is, the gateway to the Highlands, as the land to East and West, with mountainous terrain and wide rivers, makes access to the North difficult. Whoever controlled Stirling, controlled Scotland.

So, in 1314 Robert the Bruce occupied Stirling Castle and prepared for battle. One clever idea he had rendered the English army's greatest threat – the cavalry – ineffective. By having hundreds of holes a few feet wide dug in the battlefield, he ensured that their horses could not charge without stumbling and breaking their legs. The English cavalry was funnelled into approaching on a narrow path, making them easy to attack.

So it came to pass, that on 24th June 1314, Robert the Bruce's army defeated the English in The Battle of Bannockburn. It was a major victory and a turning point in the struggle for independence.

In 1320 Scotland declared itself independent and, in 1328, England grudgingly recognised the fact.

Robert the Bruce (1274-1329) is commemorated on the Clydesdale Bank Twenty Pound Sterling note with a head and shoulders portrait of him in battle dress. The note also features a smaller hologram of him set in a cobweb with a spider crawling. Paper banknotes are being replaced with polymer ones and this year The Clydesdale Bank has issued a new, redesigned, £20 note: the picture is an upward-angled, close up of Robert the Bruce's head, and the spider and web still feature.

The new polymer note:

Images used by kind permission of Clydesdale Bank

The legend has it that in his darkest hour, having been defeated in six battles against the English, Robert the Bruce sat alone in a cave in despair and on the verge of giving up. Then, a spider caught his eye as it tried to spin its cobweb across the cave entrance. The web broke, but the spider just shrugged and started again. The spider tried and failed six times to spin its web across the entrance. Then, on the seventh try, succeeded. Robert the Bruce took this as a lesson in perseverance and it gave him the fresh impetus he needed to keep on fighting until he had achieved his goal of an independent Scotland.

Original	Modern Translation
'Scots, wha hae wi Wallace bled, Scots, wham Bruce has aften led, Welcome tae yer gory bed, Or tae victorie.	'Scots, who have with Wallace bled, Scots, whom Bruce has often led, Welcome to your gory bed Or to victory.
'Now's the day, an now's the hour: See the front o battle lour, See approach proud Edward's power – Chains and Slaverie.	Now's the day, and now's the hour: See the front of battle threaten, See approach proud Edward's power Chains and Slavery
'Wha will be a traitor knave? Wha will fill a coward's grave? Wha sae base as be a slave? Let him turn an flee.	'Who will be a traitor knave? Who will fill a coward's grave? Who's so base as be a slave? – Let him turn, and flee.

'Wha, for Scotland's king and law, Freedom's sword will strongly draw, Freeman stand, or Freeman fa, Let him on wi me.	'Who for Scotland's King and Law Freedom's sword will strongly draw, Freeman stand or freeman fall, Let him follow me.
'By Oppression's woes and pains, By your sons in servile chains! We will drain our dearest veins, But they shall be free.	'By Oppression's woes and pains, By your sons in servile chains, We will drain our dearest veins But they shall be free.
'Lay the proud usurpers low, Tyrants fall in every foe, Liberty's in every blow! – Let us do or dee.	'Lay the proud usurpers low, Tyrants fall in every foe, Liberty is in every blow, Let us do or die!'

Glossary
Wha hae = who have
Wham = whom
Gory = bloody
Lour = threaten
Sae base = so worthless

Commentary

The chorus is in third person but the verses are spoken by Robert the Bruce addressing the Scottish troops before the battle of Bannockburn in 1314. No one knows what Robert the Bruce really said (any more than they know what Henry V said before Agincourt) but Burns (like Shakespeare) demonstrates his powers of imagination and rhetoric here. He has Robert the Bruce ask his troops - will they fight against 'chains and slavery', or would they rather be traitors or cowards? If the latter, he suggests they flee. If the former, he urges them to stay and draw their swords and fight for Freedom. To fight the oppressor is to save your children from slavery; you may die but your children will be free. Let us do or die!

This stirring song was the unofficial national anthem of Scotland, but has in recent times fallen out of favour to be replaced by 'Scotland the Brave' and even more recently by 'Flower of Scotland'. The latter song is played before every Scotland international rugby or football game and covers the same territory as 'Scots Wha Hae', referring to the victory at Bannockburn: 'And stood against him / Proud Edward's army / And sent him homeward / Tae think again!'

Robert Burns wrote the words for 'Scots Wha Hae', using the traditional Scottish tune, 'Hey Tuttie Tatie' which historians say may well have been played by Bruce's army at Bannockburn.

In a letter to his publisher George Thomson (in August 1793) Burns said he had been inspired by the 'glorious struggle for Freedom, associated with the glowing ideas of some other struggles of the same nature, not quite so ancient.'

Burns had to be circumspect, owing to the politics of the time, but his meaning is clear. The 'not quite so ancient' struggle he refers to is the French Revolution. The 'glowing ideas' can be encapsulated by the word **egalitarianism**. The aristocracy still held power in Europe but all over Europe that power was being challenged by new and 'radical' ideas. In January that same year Louis XVI had been executed and 'Scots Wha Hae' with its strong theme of fighting oppression and gaining 'liberty' is a coded sign of Burns' approval of the revolution. However, as a government employee (he became an Exciseman – a tax collector - in 1789) he could not express such sentiments directly or he would have been dismissed, or worse, tried for treason.

If Burns declared Republican or Radical sympathies openly he could suffer the same fate as a Glasgow lawyer who had recently been found guilty of *sedition* (i.e. inciting the Scottish people to oppose the government). The lawyer was sentenced to fourteen years in the convict settlement at Botany Bay, Australia.

It is notable that when Burns agreed to let the Morning Chronicle, of 8 May 1794, publish the song anonymously, it was on the basis of 'let them insert it as a thing they have met with by accident, and unknown to me.'

Robert the Bruce kills Henry de Bohun at Bannockburn

Protestants v Catholics

Henry VIII with Prince Edward and Jane Seymour

In the 1530's England was a Catholic country.

King Henry VIII changed all that.

Henry was having trouble producing a male heir to the throne, blamed his wife, and desperately needed a divorce so that he could find a more fertile woman to impregnate (he would have to marry her first to ensure a legitimate heir – 'bastards' didn't count).

Divorce was a no-no back then (and remains so to this day for devout Catholics). So, Henry, set up his own church, the Anglican Church, so that he could divorce and remarry. The problem was that Henry, with historical hindsight, appears to be the one to have fertility problems. As his desperation for an heir increased he speeded up the divorce process and some of his wives literally lost their heads. The fate of all six wives unfortunate enough to have married possibly the most physically and spiritually revolting, psychotic tyrant that has ever sat on the throne of England was: divorced, beheaded, died, divorced, beheaded, survived - which reminds me of my favourite 'Dad joke':

Why did Henry VIII have so many wives? Punchline: He liked to chop and change!

Not only did Henry anger the Pope by creating the rival Church of England; he then went one step further by declaring himself its 'Supreme Head'.

By the end of the 1530's the Church of England was up and running and the Pope had excommunicated Henry VIII from the Catholic Church.

This bothered Henry not a jot but became a big problem for English Catholics. For a devout Catholic, the Pope is the Head of the Church, so by not accepting Henry as the Head of the Church you could be construed as committing a kind of treason – especially by a psychopathic monarch. The world was not big on multiculturalism and religious tolerance back then, so if you disagreed with the prevailing ideas you didn't just get cancelled on social media – you literally lost your head. No one had much time for 'unconscious bias training', and there was no distinction between microaggressions and macroaggressions. So, it became open season on Catholics. Outspoken Catholics were tortured for a bit before having their heads chopped off and placed on spikes at the entrances to cities - and the rest were just discriminated against.

After Henry's death, England remained Anglican and Catholics remained an oppressed minority.

The *Union of the Crowns* in 1603 brought a glimmer of hope for Catholics, when King James VI of Scotland became, simultaneously, King James I of England. Unfortunately, nothing changed as James, despite being baptised a Roman Catholic, was more sympathetic to Protestantism and even went so far as to order all the Catholic priests to leave the country.

Remember, Remember, the Fifth of November

In frustration a group of 13 Catholics decided enough was enough. They felt it would be a good idea to assassinate King James I, and all the members of the House of Parliament. They hit upon the idea of blowing Parliament up (in those days there was only one House, The House of Lords, and you got a place in it by being an aristocrat). The House of Commons had not been thought of yet; there was none of this equality and democracy nonsense back then. Allow Commoners the vote? Are you crazy?

On the night of November 5th 1605 the conspirators, from their rented house next to Parliament, snuck 36 barrels of gunpowder into the cellars beneath the debating chamber. Guy Fawkes wasn't the leader, but he was the explosives expert. He was left alone overnight with the barrels, and a box of matches in order to light the fuse in the morning after the King and all the politicians had arrived.

Unfortunately, Guy was caught by guards on a routine inspection (maybe he snored too loudly) and tortured until he named his co-conspirators.

British justice wasn't as lenient in 1605 as it is today and crimes were easy to solve: if they caught you, they just tortured you until you agreed you were guilty. They were in no hurry; they had racks and thumbscrews, sharp knives and hot pokers, and they were quite happy to wait and amuse themselves until you made up your mind and confessed. They also had a lovely torture that made its way into George Orwell's **1984**: they would place a cage on your stomach, pop a hungry rat in and leave it until it ate its way to freedom through your insides. In an infamous case in Edinburgh, the hungry rat chewed into the victim's belly and was killed by his stomach acid. The torturers just left it in there to decompose, so the victim could enjoy a slow, painful death.

Once the conspirators confessed they faced the usual punishment: a trial which found them guilty and then an elaborate execution - hung and quartered (chopped into four and then the body parts distributed to four different corners of the kingdom (for the enlightenment and education of the people). Executions were usually public. Even up until Charles Dickens' time families made a day of it, taking the grandparents, the children, and a picnic hamper - public execution was the 17th century version of Strictly Come Dancing or The X Factor.

As you might have guessed from my 'gallows humour', in Britain we are quite cynical about politicians. Perhaps that's why we have a Guy Fawkes night every 5th November? We build bonfires, set off fireworks, and burn an effigy of Guy Fawkes which we call the 'Guy'- we love a bit of gunpowder and treason. In the past it might have been to celebrate Guy Fawkes' failure, but nowadays I think it is more to celebrate his attempt! At any rate it gives me another opportunity for a joke: 'Who was the last man to enter the Houses of Parliament with good intentions?' Answer: 'Guy Fawkes.'

Guy Fawkes' iconic image, signifying the ultimate rebellion against authority, remains relevant today. It was used in Alan Moore's graphic novel, and the subsequent film, **V for Vendetta**. The face mask worn by the anti-hero of the piece has also been co-opted by the activist group, **Anonymous Hackers**, who engage in various illegal and seditious activities such as hacking into government computers.

Back to 1605. After the failure of 'the gunpowder plot', Catholics had it worse than ever. New laws were passed to bar them from practising law, serving as officers in the armed services, or voting. They didn't get the vote back for over 200 years.

My grandfather on my mother's side, Willie Martin, born well before political correctness sucked the life out of the universe, used to roll his eyes when the Catholics in the flat upstairs were noisy. Then he'd sigh and mutter, 'Damned blue lips and hairy backs!' We had no idea what he meant, but my mum worked it out one day, long after he had passed away and gone to Calvinist heaven. She guessed that it was a reference to the Catholic practices of kissing cold statues of the Virgin Mary, and wearing hair shirts for penance.

Cavaliers, Roundheads, and the Divine Right of Kings

In the English Civil War of 1641 to 1652, the Cavaliers were the Royalists who supported Charles I, and the Roundheads were the Parliamentarians who supported Oliver Cromwell.

'Roundheads' wasn't a reference to some kind of genetic abnormality, but a pejorative nickname for Cromwell's puritanical supporters, who wore their hair short. In contrast, the Cavaliers had long hair (or long curly wigs) and sported big, floppy hats with feathers - and looked altogether more dashing.

Unfortunately – perhaps - wars are not won by the most stylish, and the Cavaliers were defeated and the monarchy overthrown.

This was a seismic event in British history. Up until Charles I monarchs had absolute power which was succinctly expressed in the phrase, 'the Divine Right of Kings'.

The worldview then (and for hundreds, if not hundreds of thousands, of years) bore no resemblance to the politics of today. There was no theory of social equality, rather an acceptance of a hierarchical society where everyone (the high and the low) knew their place. At the very top in heaven (the spiritual realm) was God and various tiers of angels and then, on earth (the material realm) the top of the pyramid was The King (or Queen), who was regarded as God's representative on earth. Everyone was subordinate to the monarch and knew their station in the hierarchy (these ideas are fully explained in the book: Tillyard, E. M. (1942) **The Elizabethan World Picture).**

It followed then that, because the monarch was divinely appointed, **regicide** (the killing of a king) was a crime against God and would lead to complete anarchy.

This is very clear in Shakespeare's plays where all hell is let loose when a king is murdered. For example, in **Hamlet** the hero states, 'there is something *rotten* in the state of Denmark'. The King's murder causes the whole country to rot from the top down. Unnatural events occur, such as the dead king's ghost appearing and asking Hamlet to avenge him. Chaos and confusion follow: Ophelia commits suicide; Hamlet kills Polonius; and, at the end of the play, the country is invaded by Norway, and Hamlet dies, along with his guilty mother and uncle.

In **Macbeth,** the eponymous hero kills the king and takes his place. Again, the country descends into supernatural evil and disorder. King Macbeth and Lady Macbeth are consumed with guilt. Macbeth becomes increasingly tyrannical, taking bad advice from witches, and going on a brutal killing spree to keep power. Lady Macbeth loses her mind and commits suicide. The country is plunged into war, and the divine order is only restored when Macbeth is killed and the rightful heir takes the throne.

Interestingly, the concept of **Divine Right** is so embedded in the British psyche that even after the death penalty was abolished in 1965, you could still be hanged for **regicide**. This law was only changed, and capital punishment fully abolished, more than thirty years later, in 1998.

Now, Charles I had an unfortunate relationship with Parliament, and suspended it a few times (in 1625 and 1629) because it dared to argue with him, mainly about giving him the money he wanted for wars.

Parliament wanted more power and the uneasy relationship between parliament and The Crown came to a head with the **Civil War in 1641**. The winners, Oliver Cromwell and The Roundheads, abolished the monarchy and had Charles executed in 1649.

However, as history shows us over and over with tedious predictability, the solution was worse than the problem and Cromwell (titled *The Lord Protector*) was even more of a tyrant than the King had been. In fact, he was so terrible that when he died the People had reached the conclusion that maybe the 'Divine right of Kings' wasn't such a bad idea after all and could they have it back, please?

So, after Cromwell's death in 1658, Parliament decided to restore the monarchy. Charles II took the throne in 1660.

However, the modern age had begun and the balance of power continued to drift from Monarch to Parliament. It was a gradual process which led to today's situation where the Queen is the titular Head of State but does not exercise power or influence over parliamentary democracy. The Divine Right of Kings has ceased to apply and is only symbolic in that the Queen has to sign and therefore formally approve every Act of Parliament and also, after General Elections, the newly elected Prime Minister has to take a limousine to Buckingham Palace and ask the Queen for her permission to form a new government.

The Rise of the Jacobites

By 1688, we have a Catholic King back in charge of what has now been a Protestant country for 150 years: James Stuart (King James II of England, and also King James VII of Scotland).

His followers became known as 'Jacobites' because 'Jacobus' was the Latin name for James. So a Jacobite was a follower of James Stuart, King James II of England (also, King James VII of Scotland).

King James II was not popular in a Protestant England fearing a resurgence of Catholicism. So, in 1688 Parliament invited William of Orange, a protestant Dutchman (who was married to James' daughter Mary), to invade. (N.B. Orange was a feudal state in Provence, France - not a reference to fruit or fake tan). Arriving with a huge armada, William won a decisive battle in 1689 forcing James to flee the country. The English Parliament happily gave the throne to protestant William to rule England, Scotland and Ireland jointly with his wife Mary.

The deposed King James II, was welcomed by his cousin Louis XIV, and settled into exile in Catholic France. On 16th September 1701, he died.

James' son, also named James (born in 1688, and now 13 years old), asserted his right to the English throne as James III of England (and James VIII of Scotland). Although he had little or no support in Protestant England, he did have support from the Scottish Highlanders (who were mainly Catholic) and from his relative Louis XIV.

Support for rebellion grew after one more famous incident with far reaching repercussions: the Act of Union (1707).

The Act of Union (1707)

The kingdoms of Scotland and England were joined by **The Act of Union** in 1707, much to the annoyance of many Scots who felt that they had been betrayed by their own aristocracy. Indeed, there is a list of how much each Scottish aristocrat was paid for voting in favour of the union.

It was clear bribery.

Let us name and shame.

Here is an extract (the full list can be found at:
https://historum.com/threads/parcel-o-rogues.5772/

Earl of Cromarty: received £300. In 2006, this was worth £41,798
Lord Preston Hall: received £200. In 2006, this was worth £27,865
Lord Ormiston: received £200. In 2006, this was worth £27,865
Duke of Montrose: received £200. In 2006, this was worth £27,865

Earl of Forfar: received £100. In 2006, this was worth £13,932
Sir Kenneth MacKenzie: received £100. In 2006, this was worth £13,932
Earl of Glencairn: received £100. In 2006, this was worth £13,932
Earl of Kintore: received £200. In 2006, this was worth £27,865
Earl of Findlator: received £100. In 2006, this was worth £13,932
Lord Forbes: received £50. In 2006, this was worth £6,966
John Muir, Provost of Ayr: received £100. In 2006, this was worth £13,932
Earl of Seafield, Lord Chancellor: £490. In 2006, this was worth £68,266
Marquis of Tweedale: received £1000. In 2006, this was worth £139,328
Duke of Roxburgh: received £500. In 2006, this was worth £69,664
Lord Elibank: received £50. In 2006, this was worth £6,966
Lord Banff: received £11-2/-. In 2006, this was worth £1,550
The Commisioner for Equippage & Daily Allowance (Duke of Queensberry): received £12,325. In 2006, this was worth £1,717,220

The money conversions given above (multiplying the 1707 figure by 139.32) strike me as too low and I set out an alternative method in Appendix 2.

As with most historical events there are disputes between historians. However, there seems to be general agreement that the majority of the Scottish people (perhaps as much as 80% of them) did not want a union with England and viewed the noble signatories to the deal as traitors. In an age when the ordinary man could not vote, never mind hold political office, the members of the Scottish Parliament were all rich and important men. Burns wrote a song in 1791 describing these signatories in scathing terms as 'a parcel o' rogues' selling out Scotland for 'English gold'.

The song appeared anonymously in The Scots Musical Museum, 1792. If Burns had put his name to it then he may have faced charges of sedition and been jailed or worse. He had already been investigated and warned that as an Excise man he was not allowed to express anti-government sentiments. Here is the song:

A Parcel O' Rogues

Fareweel to a' our Scottish fame,
Fareweel our ancient glory;
Fareweel ev'n to the Scottish name,
Sae fam'd in martial story.
Now Sark rins over Solway sands,
An' Tweed rins to the ocean,
To mark where England's province stands-
Such a parcel of rogues in a nation!

What force or guile could not subdue,
Thro' many warlike ages,
Is wrought now by a coward few,
For hireling traitor's wages.
The English stell we could disdain,
Secure in valour's station;
But English gold has been our bane-
Such a parcel of rogues in a nation!

O would, ere I had seen the day
That Treason thus could sell us,
My auld grey head had lien in clay,
Wi' Bruce and loyal Wallace!
But pith and power, till my last hour,
I'll mak this declaration;
We're bought and sold for English gold-
Such a parcel of rogues in a nation!

This lyric captures perfectly the sentiments of the majority of ordinary Scots, and is one reason that Burns is hailed as a 'man of the people'. The language is plain and simple, and the meaning clear.

However, the title needs some analysis.

This was a strict hierarchical society where criticism of your social superiors, your 'betters', was dangerous and could lead to the charge of sedition (the act of encouraging rebellion). At the very least, it might damage your employment prospects, patronage, and position in 'polite society'. In an age of deference, Burns' use of the word 'rogues' is bold. Perhaps by 1791, at the height of his fame, emboldened by his status as the recognised Scottish national poet, he felt secure enough to comment. Further, having travelled to Edinburgh and mixed with the higher echelons of society, he had been unimpressed.

The most interesting word in the title is 'parcel'. Why this unusual choice? We might expect, a 'group' of 'rogues'; after all, we wouldn't say a 'parcel' of doctors, or a 'parcel' of soldiers. At first, taking 'parcel' in its modern usage as a wrapped up gift or purchase I thought Burns usage was quite unique. In the modern sense it is fitting as this group of 'rogues' had sold Scotland to England as if it was a gift: literally, signed, sealed and delivered. However, consulting the Dictionary of the Scots Language made it clear that 'parcel' was a word, frequently used in agriculture (so Burns would be very familiar with it) meaning 'a small section of land' or, in wider usage:

'1.a. A distinct part or section of an account.
b. A part or instalment of a complete payment
https://dsl.ac.uk/entry/dost/parcell

So, the word was in common use to describe a financial transaction and this is indeed the theme of the poem. The 'parcel o' rogues' were a group of aristocrats who had been bought by the English 'For hireling traitor's wages', and sold Scotland in an act of 'Treason'.

Burns political sympathies here are quite clear.

The enforced Act of Union, bought with bribery, has been a source of anger ever since and the growth of the SNP (the Scottish National Party) put pressure on the British parliament and resulted in a devolved Scottish Parliament being opened in 2004, granting limited powers and being subordinate to the United Kingdom Parliament based in Westminster, London.

However, this limited, devolved power led to further demands for independence and a referendum was held in 2014.

The people of Scotland voted, by 55% to 45% in favour of staying in the United Kingdom.

Today, in 2020, the SNP (the Scottish National Party) is the largest political party in Scotland, and was elected in 2019 on the mandate that it would push for another independence referendum, despite the No vote in 2014. One of their main arguments for a second referendum being that Brexit meant that Scotland, who voted overwhelmingly in remaining part of the European Union, has been forced out of the EU by England.

At present, it is unclear whether or not the SNP will succeed in delivering another referendum or, even if they do, whether or not it will overturn the No vote. However, what is clear is that many Scots are unhappy and feel much the same about the Union as they did in Burns' day.

The Jacobite Rebellions
1708, 1715 and 1719

Now, James' support grew because Scotland had effectively been turned into a colony of England. The 1707 Act of Union saw Scotland's Parliament disbanded, and all political power shifted to Westminster. The Scottish people were suffering economically and politically and they wanted their Parliament back, they wanted their country back, and many even wanted their Catholic King back.

The Jacobites were there to oblige.

The Jacobites believed in the Divine Right of Kings. As God's representative on earth the King could never be deposed by man or parliament. It follows then, that James II's deposition was illegal and unholy – a crime against both Man and God. Further, the Stuart line was backed by Catholic countries such as France, Spain and Ireland who would prefer a Catholic on the throne, and therefore officially recognised James II's son as King James III.

So, the unrest in Scotland and Catholic Europe continued and there were Jacobite uprisings in 1708 and again in 1715. But James' armies were defeated.

James III tried again in 1719 but, once more, was defeated. After this last attempt he was given refuge in Rome by the Pope where, with his court, he lived out the rest of his life in luxurious exile. His efforts to regain the crown had earned him the nickname in England, 'The Old Pretender'.

Bonnie Prince Charlie and the 1745 Rebellion

Still the Jacobite cause was not done. Discontent with the Union and the usurping of the Stuart line simmered on and the final, most successful, and most famous rebellion began when James III's 25 year old son, Bonnie Prince Charlie, landed alone in the north of Scotland on a mission to claim the throne for its rightful heir, his father.

Charlie raised an army of Highlanders loyal to the Jacobite cause. Then he marched them south, and defeated the English government forces at **The Battle of Prestonpans** in September 1745.

Scotland's capital city, Edinburgh, opened up its gates to receive the Jacobite victors. Edinburgh Castle remained impregnable, under government control, but this was a minor inconvenience as the people of Edinburgh gave Charlie and his Highlanders a hero's welcome. He took up residence in Holyrood Palace, and had his portrait painted by famous Scottish painter, Allan Ramsay. This portrait was 'lost' in 1746 and was only rediscovered in 2009, by the brilliant detective work of an intrepid art historian called Bendor Grosvenor. He finally tracked the portrait down to Gosford House, the stately home of the Earl of Wemyss in Longniddry, a village a few miles from the site of the Battle of Prestonpans. The portrait is now on display at The Scottish National Gallery in Queen's Street, Edinburgh.

With Edinburgh secured, the Bonnie Prince proclaimed that Scotland was once again an independent nation under the reign of his father, King James VIII of Scotland.

In six weeks the Jacobite army was on the march, heading south to take the city of London and re-establish the Stuart dynasty in England. Charlie believed it was his destiny and that God was on his side.

The lost portrait of Bonnie Prince Charlie by Allan Ramsay

However, conquering England was not going to be so easy. The army got as far as Derby where they were given false information by an English spy in their midst that their route was blocked by a large English force. The truth was that there was no army, the road was open all the way to London, and the English were in disarray. Further, the Catholic French were preparing to invade to help Charlie and, 126 miles away in London, King George II was in a panic, hurriedly packing his bags to flee the country.

Charlie wanted to press on to London, but he was overruled by his chief tacticians, and so the Scots army about turned and headed back north.

The fate of the Scottish nation, indeed the whole United Kingdom, turned on one, uncorroborated lie.

The retreat was a disastrous mistake. It gave the English forces time to regroup and the Jacobite army shrank as tired, demoralised Highlanders drifted off back to their homes in the north.

The final showdown came at Culloden on 16th April 1746. The exhausted and depleted Jacobites were outnumbered and outmanoeuvred by a fresh and well-equipped English army.

It was a massacre.

The aftermath of Culloden was even worse than the battle. The English were led by the Duke of Cumberland who earned the nickname, 'The Butcher'. He was desperate to capture the Bonnie Prince and make him less bonnie. His army spread throughout Scotland hunting down the rebels, torturing locals for information as to Charlie's whereabouts, raping and murdering women, and killing children as they went.

Despite the cruelty of the English, or perhaps because of it, the people of Scotland were loyal to Charlie. The government put a £30,000 price tag on his head (in today's money that would be anywhere between £5 million and £45 million – see Appendix 2 for a full explanation).

But no one betrayed the Prince. He was given safe passage throughout Scotland, eventually reaching the West coast, escaping 'over the sea to Skye' (immortalised in 'The Skye boat song') and from there back to France.

The ordinary people left behind paid a high price. The English authorities decided it was time to teach these unruly barbarians a lesson. So, the kilt was banned and the 'Highland Clearances' began, a policy of forcibly removing families from the land and sending them abroad (a literal 'clearing' of the Highlands). Many Highlanders were slaughtered or exiled, all in order to break up the rebellious Scottish Clans once and for all.

Burns and the Jacobites

Burns was born in 1759, only 14 years after the Jacobite Rebellion of 1745.

As stated in Chapter 1, support for the Jacobites during the Rebellion had affected Burns' family directly, costing them much of their wealth.

So, Burns was not an admirer of the Hanoverian King George III, but knew he could not openly express Jacobite sympathies. He was able to do so in 'Charlie, He's My Darling' as the song already existed as a long 'street' ballad in various versions, allowing Burns to claim he was a collector, rather than an author. The original has not to my knowledge ever been unearthed, but if it had any political overtones Burns reworking has removed them in favour of a light, bawdy touch. It is a fine example of Burns borrowing and improving on songs existing in the oral tradition. It is unashamedly romantic, as you might expect – after all, what could be more romantic than the foppish, dandified image of the young and 'bonnie' Prince?

Charlie, He's My Darling

Original	Modern Translation
'Twas on a Monday morning, Right early in the year, That Charlie came to our town, The young **Chevalier**.	It was on a Monday morning, Very early in the year, That Charlie came to our town, The young Cavalier.
An' Charlie, he's my darling, My darling, my darling, Charlie, he's my darling, The young Chevalier.	And Charlie, he's my darling, My darling, my darling, Charlie, he's my darling, The young Cavalier.
As he was walking up the street, The city for to view, O there he spied a **bonie lass** The window looking through,	As he was walking up the street, The city for to view, O there he spied a pretty girl The window looking through,
Sae light's he jumped up the stair, And **tirl'd at the pin**; And **wha sae** ready as hersel' To let the laddie in.	So lightly he jumped up the stair, And rattled the door knob; And no one was more ready than her / To let the boy in.
He set his Jenny on his knee, All in his Highland dress; For **brawly weel he ken'd the way** To please a bonnie lass.	He set his Jenny on his knee, All in his Highland dress; For good and well he knew the way / To please a pretty girl.
It's up yon heathery mountain, An' down yon **scroggie** glen, We **daur na gang** a milking, For Charlie and his men,	It's up that heathery mountain, An' down that glen full of stunted bushes, We dare not go a milking, Because of Charlie and his men,
An' Charlie, he's my darling, My darling, my darling, Charlie, he's my darling, The young Chevalier.	And Charlie, he's my darling, My darling, my darling, Charlie, he's my darling, The young Cavalier.

Glossary

Chevalier – the French word for a knight on horseback. The English equivalent is 'Cavalier' – think 'cavalry' / horses. The word was old fashioned, even in Burns' time, and had connotations of nobility, and flamboyance. As discussed earlier, the Cavaliers in the English Civil War were the Royalists who had long hair and wore cool hats with feathers in. Their opponents, the Roundheads (as the very name suggests) had uncool, pudding bowl haircuts, and a Puritanical outlook on life that would forbid the wearing of fancy hats at rakish angles, adorned by feathers.

Bonie lass – pretty girl. This is usually spelled 'bonnie'. However, English spelling did not really begin to be standardised until Samuel Johnson's Dictionary of 1755 appeared and it does not feature Scottish Lowland Dialect words like 'bonie/bonnie'.

tirl'd at the pin – rattled the door knob
brawly – finely, handsomely

weel – well

kenn'd – knew

scroggie – having **scrogs** upon it (and a **scrog** is a short, stunted tree or bush like blackthorn or hawthorn (according to the Collins online dictionary). Also, **scrog** (according to the online Free Dictionary) is slang for having sex. How recent this usage is and whether Burns was aware of it or not I don't know. I would hazard a guess that Burns did know the alternative, slang meaning, and deliberately placed the word there to emphasise the sexual theme of the song.

daur na gang – dare not go

Commentary

The song could be set in any (or every) town that Charlie and his men passed through as the phrase 'right early in the year' was chosen for its sound, not its historical accuracy (Charlie had landed in Scotland on 23rd July 1745). But the word 'city' is used and it is not a huge stretch of the imagination to visualise the scene where Charlie and his soldiers swagger into Edinburgh puffed up with the success of their resounding victory at Prestonpans, turning the heads of the young ladies and immediately indulging in sexual escapades.

Burns depicts a swashbuckling Bonnie Prince Charlie, with the emphasis on his attractiveness and sexual prowess. The jaunty rhythm and the details of Charlie's amorous encounter create a light, comic image of one of the most romantic events in Scotland's history.

Ye Jacobites by Name

Burns' grandfather, Robert Burnes (spelling was not standardised and the family hadn't dropped the 'e' yet) had Jacobite connections, and failed to sign a petition of loyalty to the King. Therefore, he was punished by having many of his assets taken by the government.

So, Burns growing up would have been familiar with his family history, and any sympathy he had with the Jacobite cause would be tempered by this knowledge. He knew that it was dangerous to express pro-Jacobite sentiments, and he was well aware of the damage done to Scotland as a result of the 1745 rebellion. This next song is very much an anti-war song.

Original	Modern Standard English
Ye Jacobites by name, give an ear, give an ear, Ye Jacobites by name, give an ear; Ye Jacobites by name, Your fautes I will proclaim, Your doctrines I maun blame - you shall hear!	You Jacobites by name, listen, listen, You Jacobites by name, listen; You Jacobites by name, Your faults I will shout out, Your doctrines I must blame - you shall hear!
What is Right and what is Wrang, by the law, by the law? What is Right and what is Wrang by the law? What is Right, and what is Wrang? A short sword, and a lang, A weak arm and a strang, for to draw!	What is Right and what is Wrong, by the law, by the law? What is Right and what is Wrong by the law? What is Right, and what is Wrong? A short sword, and a long, A weak arm and a strong, for to draw!
What makes heroic strife, famed afar, famed afar? What makes heroic strife famed afar?	What is the outcome of heroic struggle, famed afar, famed afar? What is the outcome of heroic struggle famed afar?

What makes heroic strife? To whet th' Assassin's knife, Or haunt a Parent's life, wi' bluidy war? Then let your schemes alone, in the State, in the State, Then let your schemes alone in the state. Then let your schemes alone, Adore the rising sun, And leave a man undone, to his fate.	What is the outcome of heroic struggle? To sharpen the Assassin's knife, Or haunt a Parent's life, with bloody war? Then leave your schemes alone, in the State, in the State. Then leave your schemes alone in the state. Then leave your schemes alone, Adore the rising sun, And leave a man ruined, to his fate.

Commentary

The song opens with the chorus which appears to be critical of the Jacobites, the speaker asking them to listen ('give an ear') while he questions their 'doctrines' and beliefs.

However, he fails to do this in the first verse. Instead he questions morality, asking 'what is right and what is wrong? By the law'. There is no moral certainty here; he is not asking what is **truly** right and what is **truly** wrong but is, instead, suggesting that moral judgements are decided by man-made law.

After the Jacobite uprising (1745) and the French Revolution (1789) the authorities cracked down on anyone showing support for forces that sought to upset the established order, and Burns had to couch his views in a coded and highly ambiguous way if he was to avoid arrest and ruin. This verse could be interpreted as critical of the government and the laws it brought in to stifle Jacobite support.

Here the speaker does not address the Jacobites. So who is he addressing? He seems to be addressing all of us; to make us question the law and not jump to easy conclusions or lend our support to one side or another.

In the second verse, Burns questions the idea of heroism. Fighting for a cause, leads to the ignoble actions of the assassin or to pointless deaths. Here the parents have to suffer the real consequences of an ideology, such as Jacobitism, that results in war.

In the final verse, Burns calls for an end to the political scheming that led to the death and destruction of 1745. Instead, he argues that we should take pleasure in nature, in the 'rising sun', and leave 'a man undone, to his fate'. Perhaps 'undone' refers to a Jacobite facing execution or even to Bonnie Prince Charlie himself, and the Speaker of the poem is suggesting that we would be best to give up the cause and forget him.

Burns has a point, the Jacobite cause had brought nothing but misery to Scotland; the 'Highland Clearances' that followed has been described by some historians as ethnic cleansing or genocide, but this has been disputed and probably refuted. What is more certain is that the Clearances destroyed a way of life - the ancient clan culture.

If there is a plus side to the Jacobite rebellion and the Highland Clearances, it is that Scots were scattered all over the world and their ingenuity and character led to progress everywhere they went (especially in the USA and Canada).

The **Battle of Culloden**, oil on canvas, David Morier, 1746, Royal Collection Trust

Chapter 7

The Politics of Egalitarianism

'A Man's a Man for A' That'
(also know as, 'Is There for Honest Poverty')
'Auld Lang Syne'

'While Europe's eye is fix'd on mighty things,
The fate of empires and the fall of kings;
While quacks of State must each produce his plan,
And even children lisp the Rights of Man;
Amid this mighty fuss just let me mention,
The Rights of Woman merit some attention.'

We are all products of the times we live in. We are raised in a society, a culture, that shapes our identity and thought. It can be difficult for a modern audience to fully appreciate and understand that ideas and beliefs today are neither universal nor permanent. Anyone with half a brain living in the insanity of 2020 has probably reached the conclusion that morality borders on the whimsical and farcical. Or perhaps that is the cynical view of an older person as he sees the ideas of the illogical, but ever so feeling, younger generation sweep away the past as they remould reality and society to conform to their own prejudices. It was ever thus.

In Robert Burns' lifetime (the mid to late 18th century) society was shaped very differently from today. There was a strict hierarchy and the 'social mobility' that sociologists like to talk about was somewhere between negligible and non-existent. I was reminded of this recently watching the television series starring Sean Bean, based on Bernard Cornwell's **Sharpe** novels. Set not long after Burns' death, in the Napoleonic Wars (1803-1815), it shows how the hero, Sharpe, is constantly in conflict with both his social superiors and men of his own class. The reason for this is that Sharpe is a working class man raised from the ranks to be an officer. This rarely happened and such men were both mistrusted by the working class soldiers under them, as well as the rich, aristocratic officers around and above them. This was an age where men bought their ranks, not earned them - truly a case of 'white privilege'. A recurring insult aimed at Sharpe throughout, is that he is 'not a proper officer', and as he is 'not a gentleman' he is not fit to lead.

    This social reality dogged Burns' life and thought. When, at the height of his fame, he became the darling of the Edinburgh social elite, he was made painfully aware of his status. He made many withering comments in his letters about the 'blockheads' (one of his favourite words) he encountered among the aristocracy. He quickly realised that wealth and status did not equate with intelligence or worth. If he had a chip on his shoulder before Edinburgh, it became cemented there during his first stay in the winter of 1786. Despite his 'rock star' status, his wit and charm, his abundant charisma, and his practised ease with Ayrshire women, Burns was not able to gratify himself sexually with the rank conscious, upper class females of Edinburgh. He had to content himself with servant girls.

    This is not to say that Burns didn't try to penetrate the class barrier (so to speak). He clearly desired Mrs. Nancy McLehose and entered a lengthy campaign of courtship. However, despite the teasing, the romantic love letters, the intimate evenings alone together in her candle lit room, the affair did not end in the usual consummation. It appears from the letters that Nancy had religious and moral objections to a physical relationship and her desire for Burns was outweighed by her concern for her reputation in the small, social world of upper class Edinburgh. She channelled her desire into fantasy and, it appears, Burns (who already had pregnant Jean Armour, dutifully waiting at home in Ayrshire, and was sexually active with at least one Edinburgh servant) was able, without too much sacrifice, to fantasise with her in creating a pure and chaste love.

Putting matters of the heart aside, in Burns' day the class system dominated education and government. Peasants throughout Europe were largely uneducated and reading and writing was a preserve of the ruling class. Further voting rights were not universal but restricted to a small, privileged percentage of the population. However, across Europe, things were beginning to change, and revolution was in the air.

In Scotland, things were already changing. As a Scot I am happy to argue that the Scots created the modern world, this tiny nation punching well above its weight in ingenuity and invention. Examples abound:

Sir Walter Scott – the historical novel;
James Watt – the steam engine (the unit of power, the watt, is named after him)
Sir James Young Simpson – chloroform as an anaesthetic
Lord Kelvin – the second law of thermodynamics
Kirkpatrick MacMillan – the bicycle
John Boyd Dunlop – the modern, pneumatic tire
Sir James Dewar – the vacuum flask
Adam Smith – economics (see **The Wealth of Nations**)
John Logie Baird – the television
Alexander Graham Bell – the telephone
Sir Robert Alexander Watson-Watt - radar
Stevenson – the lighthouse
MacIntosh – the raincoat
Sir Alexander Fleming – penicillin

Scots also invented: the SAS; the flushing toilet; the refrigerator; the toaster; modern geology; golf; The Bank of England; criminal fingerprinting; logarithms; decimal points; the hypodermic syringe; the video game Grand Theft Auto; and hypnotherapy.

https://www.scotsman.com/arts-and-culture/ten-surprising-scottish-inventions-1494798

and

https://theculturetrip.com/europe/united-kingdom/scotland/articles/25-awesome-things-scotland-gave-the-world/

So, how did this happen? Is it because the Scots are a superior race and can outthink every other?

I do like to think so.

Sadly, it might not be true – and even if it were, saying so would get me cancelled on social media.

The truth lies in education. In the 18th and 19th centuries Scotland had the best education system in the world.

Education in the 18th Century.

Nowadays, we take for granted that we are educated to a high level. In Britain today education is compulsory from the age of 5 until the age of 18.

However, in Burns time the aristocracy ruled and the majority of people were uneducated peasants, most barely able to read and write.

You may also have noted, that in the list of Scottish achievers given in the last section, they were all male. The reason for this is quite simple: women were second class citizens. Scotland, like the rest of Europe, had values based on Christianity and women were regarded as inferior to men. Women were expected to stay at home, have babies, do the cooking, and look after the house. They were not expected to worry their 'pretty little heads' about 'man stuff' like reading and writing. Today, most Western liberals would see this as unbelievably sexist but Burns, like all men of his era, was born and raised with these attitudes and beliefs and it, perhaps, makes his treatment of some women understandable if not excusable.

According to Mackie (in Chapter 9) the census of 1786 showed that, in England, only 10% of the population could read. A similar level of literacy could be found in other European countries.

Knox's reforms in 1560-1561 included the positive one of setting up universal education in every Scottish parish (as earlier mentioned) – a policy which became embedded in Education Acts and came to fruition in the 18th and 19th centuries,

However, Scotland was exceptional. The same census that Mackie cites, showed that 79% of the male population were literate. This was a direct result of the Scotland Education Act of 1616 (and another in 1696), which legislated the setting up of a school in every parish to teach reading and writing to all. This initiative was Calvinist driven with the aim being to spread the word of God to all: learn to read so that you can read The Bible. Fees were charged but these were low, affordable, and, as a consequence, Scottish peasants became the best educated peasants in Europe. Daniel Defoe stated that, whereas England was a land 'full of ignorance', in Scotland the 'poorest people have their children taught and instructed.'

The democratising effect of this shouldn't be underestimated. In England, university education could only be accessed by the upper class. In Scotland, the poorest, working class child, if academically successful, could attend university. Even today, university education is free in Scotland (for Scots and anyone else who has lived in the country for three years or more) whereas in England students have to saddle themselves with lifelong debt.

In the 18th century, basic skills such as reading and writing were in short supply worldwide so the high percentage of Scots possessing them were in great demand. Many Scots emigrated to England and the colonies to become managers and administrators. Even to this day the Scottish education system enjoys a high regard, still bathing in the glow of its 18th century reputation.

Democracy in the 18th Century

Another big difference between now and then is that Britain was not a democracy as we know it today. Men over the age of 21 could vote, but only if they were wealthy or owned property. Women were not allowed to vote at all.

In Burns' lifetime (1759 to 1796) there was very little change in the voting system. As Crawford explains, 'Ayrshire had 205 voters out of a population of 65,000; neither Burns's county nor his country was a democracy in the modern sense.' (p.110). In other words, less than 4% of the population was entitled to vote.

In the whole United Kingdom, even as late as 1866, only 1.43 million could vote out of a population of 30 million. That's less than 5%. Some democracy!

In 1867 a Parliamentary Reform Act increased this to 2.5 million by allowing men who rented to vote. That's still less than 9%.

Further, not anyone could become an MP (Member of Parliament): only men could serve in the House of Commons and House of Lords. The law changed to allow women in 1958.

Even further, The House of Lords (made up of unelected representatives – i.e. the aristocracy) could overrule any law passed by the House of Commons. This remained the case until 1911.

https://www.historylearningsite.co.uk/britain-1700-to-1900/political-changes/

It was not until the **Representation of the People Act of 1918** that **all men** over the age of 21 were given the vote. The same right was extended to women over the age of 30 who had property or had a husband who owned property.

The **Representation of the People Act of 1928** extended voting rights to **all adults** over the age of 21 (regardless of gender or wealth).

So, writing this in 2020, Britain has only been a real democracy (in the modern sense) for 92 years.

Let us summarise the state of education and democracy in Britain:

- **1616 and 1692 Scotland Education Acts**: a school in every parish to teach reading and writing to all.
- **1707 The Act of Union**: England and Scotland became joint kingdoms. The Scottish Parliament closed and power was transferred to Westminster.
- **1759** (the year of Burns birth): only wealthy or land owning men over 21 could vote. Only men could serve in the Houses of Lords and Commons and the House of Lords (made up of unelected hereditary peers) could veto any legislation passed by the House of Commons.
- **1867** Parliamentary Reform Act: men over 21 who rented land could vote, extending the vote to 2.5 million out of a population of 30 million.
- **1911**: House of Lords power curbed, so that the Lords could only delay, not overrule, the House of Commons.
- **1918 Representation of the People Act: all men** over the age of 21 were given the vote. The vote was also extended to women over the age of 30 who had property or had a husband who owned property.
- **1928 Representation of the People Act: all adults** over the age of 21 (regardless of gender or wealth) could vote.

Burns and the Zeitgeist

The British establishment had survived the Civil War of 1641 and the Jacobite Rebellion of 1745. Abroad, however, the old world order was under threat. In 1775 America decided to cease being a colony of Britain. The ensuing War of Independence rumbled on from 1775 to 1783. America formally declared independence on 4th July 1776 (when Burns was seventeen). It decided it was done with unelected monarchs and chose to be a **republic**:

a country without a king or queen, usually governed by elected representatives of the people and a president
https://dictionary.cambridge.org/dictionary/english/republic

In France the aristocrats' time was also up: revolutionaries seized power and declared the country a Republic in 1792. The revolutionaries then rounded up the French aristocracy and chopped their heads off with the brand new machine, the guillotine. This made the aristocracy of countries like Britain very nervous; they worried that their peasants might draw inspiration from their French neighbours.

N.B. The French continued to use the guillotine until 1977.

With the publication of Thomas Paine's **The Rights of Man** in 1791 (in defence of the French Revolution and championing dangerous egalitarian notions, such as free speech, equality, and brotherhood, along with practical plans for universal education, pensions and social welfare for the poor) the seeds of the modern age were well and truly sewn, and the spirit of the age had been articulated.

The Rights of Man was a best-seller but the elites considered it to be dangerously subversive (of their interests) so they had Thomas Paine tried for 'seditious libel' against the government.

But it was too late, Pandora's box was open and there was no shutting it now; 'the spirit of the age' could probably be summed up in one word: *egalitarianism*.

Egalitarianism

The Merriam-Webster online dictionary identifies the first use of the word ***egalitarianism*** as being 1874, which is long after Burns' death:

1: a belief in human equality especially with respect to social, political, and economic affairs

2: a social philosophy advocating the removal of inequalities among people

https://www.merriam-webster.com/dictionary/egalitarianism

Egalitarianism is at the core, the heart of **Democracy** and **Republicanism**. It underpins western civilisation and is embedded in ideas such as **equal rights** (regardless of race or gender); **equality before the law**; and **equality of opportunity.**

Egalitarianism is enshrined in the American constitution because, in theory at least, every American citizen, whatever their background, gender or race, has an equal opportunity to become President of the United States.

The American Declaration of Independence (1776) began:

We hold these truths to be self-evident, that all men are created equal, that they are endowed by their Creator with certain unalienable Rights, that among these are Life, Liberty and the pursuit of Happiness.

This same egalitarian philosophy inspired President Abraham Lincoln to abolish slavery in The South, triggering a Civil War. Here is the opening sentence of his **Gettysburg Address** of 1864:

Four score and seven years ago our fathers brought forth on this continent, a new nation, conceived in Liberty, and dedicated to the proposition that all men are created equal.
http://www.abrahamlincolnonline.org/lincoln/speeches/gettysburg.htm

Burns worldwide popularity owes much to the fact that he was a poet of his time, a poet who captured the zeitgeist. The word egalitarianism may not have come into use in his lifetime, but the idea was there, and Burns gave it its finest expression in this, his most famous egalitarian song.

A Man's a Man for A' That

Also known by its first line, 'Is There For Honest Poverty', the song 'was published anonymously in *The Glasgow Magazine* because Burns dare not put his name to it for fear of reprisals from the authorities.

Some have argued that Burns was a socialist and a supporter of the French revolution, but his politics were not as clear cut as that. Like Shakespeare, what shines through his work is his humanity, his innate sense of justice, not any particular political philosophy.

Nonetheless, the song has been appropriated as an anthem by politicians and was sung by Sheena Wellington at the opening of the Scottish Parliament in May 1999, and again by Midge Ure in 2016.

The song is also quoted on the crest of the SQA (the Scottish Qualifications Authority): 'pride o' worth'.

Burns wrote to Thomson in Jan 1795:

A critic on songs has said that love and wine are the exclusive themes for songwriting. The following is on neither subject, and consequently is no song, but it will be allowed, I think, to be two or three pretty good prose thoughts inverted into rhyme.

A Man's a Man for A' That

Original	Modern Translation
Is there, for honest poverty That hangs his head, and a' that; The coward slave, we pass him by, We dare be poor for a' that! For a' that, and a' that, Our toils obscure, and a' that, The rank is but the guinea's stamp, The Man's the **gowd** for a' that.	Is there, for honest poverty That hangs his head, and all that; The coward slave, we pass him by, We dare be poor for all that! For all that, and all that, Our toils obscure, and all that, The rank is but the guinea's stamp, The Man's the **gold** for all that.
What though on **hamely fare** we dine, Wear **hoddin gray**, and a' that; **Gie** fools their silks, and knaves their wine, A man's a man, for a' that! For a' that, and a' that, Their tinsel show, and a' that; The honest man, though e'er sae	What though on **homely food** we dine, Wear **a course gray cloth**, and all that; **Give** fools their silks, and knaves their wine, A man's a man, for all that! For all that, and all that, Their tinsel show, and all that; The honest man, though ever so

poor, Is king o' men for a' that!	poor, Is king o' men for all that!
Ye see yon **birkie, ca'd** a lord, Wha struts, and stares, and a' that; Though hundreds worship at his word, He's but a **coof** for a' that. For a' that, and a' that, His riband, star, and a' that, The man of independent mind, He looks and laughs at a' that.	You see that **arrogant fellow, called** a lord, Who struts, and stares, and all that; Though hundreds worship at his word, He's but a **fool** for all that. For all that, and all that, His ribbon, star, and all that, The man of independent mind, He looks and laughs at all that.
A king can make a belted knight, A marquis, duke, and a' that, But an honest man's **aboon** his might, **Guid** faith, he **maunna fa'** that! For a' that, and a' that, Their dignities, and a' that, The **pith** o' sense, and pride o' worth, Are higher ranks than a' that.	A king can make a belted knight, A marquis, duke, and all that, But an honest man's **above** his might, **Good** faith, he **must not for** all that! For all that, and all that, Their dignities, and all that, The **importance** of sense, and pride of worth, Are higher ranks than all that.
Then let us pray that come it may - As come it will for a' that - That sense and worth, o'er a' the earth, May **bear the gree**, and a' that; For a' that, and a' that, It's coming yet for a' that, That man to man, the world o'er, Shall brothers be for a' that!	Then let us pray that come it may - As come it will for all that - That sense and worth, over all the earth, May **win the victory**, and all that; For all that, and all that, It's coming yet for all that, That man to man, the world over, Shall brothers be for all that!

Commentary

The title, 'A Man's a Man For A'That' means: a man is a man, all things considered. Burns is making an argument that a man is a man, irrespective of considerations of wealth and social status.

Poetry is a compressed form of language, and so the first line makes little sense on its own: 'Is there, for honest poverty'. Burns has condensed the question: 'What can we possibly say in praise of the honest poor.' The word 'honest' gives us a big clue: for a start, we can say that the poor are honest. This may or may not be true but it does indicate that Burns is taking the side of the downtrodden. But what else is he saying? If the poor are honest, what does that say about the rich? Are they, then, not honest? Is Burns suggesting society (the establishment) is dishonest, corrupt?

To understand the meaning of the first stanza we have to expand the first few lines. Burns is asking something like: What good can be said for honest poverty if the poor man hangs his head in deference to the upper class? Such cowardly behaviour does not earn our respect ('we pass him by'). So Burns respects honesty but has no respect for the servile poor. However, the rest of the verse also expresses the sentiment that neither should we respect people of rank; they are of no more worth than the stamp of approval on a coin (a 'guinea' was a gold coin worth twenty one shillings, or £1.05 in Burns' day).

Man, regardless of social class, is worth gold.

The second stanza continues this idea. Just because a man dines and dresses simply and humbly, he is no less a man than one who dresses in fine clothes ('silk') and drinks wine. 'Tinsel' is used to show that the glamour of the rich is empty and cheap and that the poor man is just as much a 'king o' men'.

The third stanza continues to mock the aristocracy. The lord is no more than a 'birkie' and a 'coof' (an arrogant fool). A man of 'independent mind' would see through all the fancy dress (the ribbons and stars) and laugh at them.

In stanza four, Burns argues that any man can be given a title but that does not make him any better than an honest man doing the right thing ('aboon his might') or acting in good faith. Having a sense of self-worth and pride is worth more than that.

The final stanza makes a plea for 'sense and worth' to prevail across the world, for the dignity of man to overcome class divisions and for all mankind to form a universal brotherhood. It is a call for equality.

Burns is often thought of as a 'man of the people', a phrase used to describe someone who understands and sympathises with the concerns of ordinary folk, and is well-liked by them. In 'A Man's a Man for a' That' he sets forth a very Romantic conception – the innate worth and nobility of the common man. Honesty and dignity are not the preserve of the rich, the holders of rank, but essential ingredients of the soul. Democracy is coming and bringing with it universal brotherhood.

Auld Lang Syne

The final song in this collection is Burns' most poignant anthem. Its universal appeal has made Burns famous throughout the world. Here he takes the theme of brotherhood in 'A Man's a Man for a' that' and de-politicises it to create a warm, nostalgic celebration of friendship. There is no reference to class (or gender) differences, and the song is for Everyman (and Everywoman), for every race and nationality. It is sung at the end of social gatherings throughout the world. Before we go into detail, let the song speak for itself.

Original	Modern Translation
Chorus For auld lang syne, my dear, For auld lang syne, We'll tak a cup o' kindness yet, For auld lang syne.	Chorus For days long gone, my dear For days long past, We'll drink a toast of kind remembrance For days now passed
Should auld acquaintance be forgot, And never brought to min'? Should auld acquaintance be forgot, And auld lang syne?	Should old friends be forgotten and never remembered Should old friends be forgotten and the days long gone
And surely ye'll be your pint stowp! And surely I'll be mine! And we'll tak a cup o' kindness yet, For auld lang syne.	You can pay for your pint tankard and I will pay for mine We'll drink a toast of kind remembrance, For days long past
We twa hae run about the braes And pu'd the gowans fine; But we've wandered mony a weary fit Sin' auld lang syne.	We two have run about the hillsides and pulled wild daisies but now we've wandered many a weary foot From those days long gone
We twa hae paidl't i 'the burn, Frae mornin' sun till dine; But seas between us braid hae roar'd **Sin'** auld lang syne..	We two have paddled in the stream from morning until noon but seas between us have roared since those days long gone
And there's a hand, my trusty fiere! And gie's a hand o' thine! And we'll **tak** a right guid-willie-waught, For auld lang syne.	So take my hand, my trusty friend and give me your hand and we will take a hearty drink together In memory of those days long gone.

Glossary

auld = old;
min' = mind;
syne = 'since' or 'then' – pronounced like 'sign'
O' lang syne = of long ago
stowp = drinking vessel;
tak = take
twa = two;
hae = have;
braes = hills;
puil the gowans = pulled the daisies;
mony a weary fit = travelled great distances
flere = friend;
a right guidwillie waught = a goodwill drink
 dine = 'dinner time'

Commentary

Even for a Scottish child growing up in Scotland in the 1960's this was like a foreign language. Although there is something of a renaissance of Gaelic and Scottish dialect in Scotland at the moment, it was disparaged and all but obliterated when I was a child. English was the written standard and Received Pronunciation (commonly termed, 'the Queen's English') was the most prestigious dialect. Class and social status were determined largely by accent. Posh people in Edinburgh sounded English and to 'get on in life', even in Scotland, required an English Home Counties accent. At one point my parents even considered sending me to elocution lessons so that I would sound less Scottish! In 1965, George Bernard Shaw's play Pygmalion was reworked into a musical film, **My Fair Lady**. Rex Harrison plays a Professor of Elocution, who embarks on an experiment to turn a common Cockney flower girl into a lady by teaching her to speak 'properly'! He does so in response to a wager that it is an impossible task to transform someone so 'common' into a lady that will be presentable in high society. This prejudice against regional accents and dialects was embedded in society and present in the media right up until the 1960's. BBC newsreaders all spoke impeccably 'proper' or 'Queen's English' without a trace of regional accent.

It was only in the mid-60's that the class prejudice against working class dialects and accents began to change. I remember the glow of personal and national pride when Sean Connery, an 'ordinary' Edinburgh man took the role of suave, sophisticated, super agent James Bond. He was in the year below my mum at the same Edinburgh school and, on leaving, worked as a milk delivery man. To everyone's surprise he kept his Scottish accent, and still became an international superstar. The effect was like a cultural atomic bomb exploding – a great levelling had begun. Connery was soon followed by Michael Caine as Cockney spy Harry Palmer, complete with free NHS spectacles!

The BBC was slow to catch on but by the seventies Oxbridge journalists with plummy accents were being replaced by newsreaders with regional accents from all over the United Kingdom. At first it seemed unnatural, comical even. In an age of deference this was a 'drop in standards'. My mum was horrified. She worked for the BBC in Queen Street (of course) Edinburgh, as a telephonist. She answered the phone in an extravagantly posh English accent. If you imagine the Queen saying, 'Hello, BBC Switchboard, may I help you?' then you get the idea.

The phrase 'Auld lang syne' was a complete mystery to me as a child. I knew 'auld' meant old and that 'lang' meant long, but 'syne' threw me completely as it sounded like, 'sign' and 'old, long sign' didn't make any sense. Only as an adult did I learn that 'syne' means since. Even then, 'old, long since' was still a difficult concept. It means, 'times long gone by' or 'times long since passed'.

The sentiment of the song is that we should celebrate the shared experiences we had with friends in the past.

The title Burns borrowed from an older song but significantly revised the verses into the immortal version we have today. In a letter to a friend, Mrs Dunlop, he wrote:

Is not the Scotch phrase Auld lang syne, exceedingly expressive? There is an old song and tune which has often thrilled through my soul: I shall give you the verses on the other sheet. Light be the turf on the breast of the heaven-inspired poet who composed this glorious fragment.

I first encountered the song at the Edinburgh Military Tattoo. The Tattoo is held every year on the esplanade of Edinburgh Castle and attracts tourists from every land. If you ever visit Scotland in August make sure you get a ticket (they go on sale online every December). It is a fantastic spectacle, including displays of military precision and music performed by regimental bands from around the globe. My favourite moments are when busby wearing, be-kilted bagpipers and drummers march up and down the esplanade, fearsomely belting out ancient, stirring Scottish war songs. Near the evening's conclusion everyone links arms and sings, 'Auld Lang Syne' before a lone piper appears on the battlements, silhouetted against the black Edinburgh sky, to play the traditional lament, 'Sleep, Dearie, Sleep'.

A shortened version of the Edinburgh Military Tattoo is televised, but it really isn't anything like being there on a dark, cold, windy night, sitting high above the ancient city and experiencing the real, visceral beauty for yourself.

'Auld Lang Syne' is also sung at New Year throughout the world, at Burns' suppers and many other events. I have even heard that it is played at Tokyo pedestrian crossings. To test out that rumour I had a quick search on YouTube and found that Japanese stores play it at closing time:

https://www.youtube.com/watch?v=o7GxffUu7p0

I also found this:

https://www.youtube.com/watch?v=g01BgPUqTbE.

It is a farewell song from Japan called 'Hotaru no Hikari' sung to the tune of 'Auld Lang Syne'.

I failed to find any evidence of 'Auld Lang Syne' being played at Tokyo pedestrian crossings but I did find that you might cross the road in Japan to another Burns tune, 'Comin' Through the Rye':

https://www.youtube.com/watch?v=OIEpBmukDaQ

Themes of friendship and the passing of time make 'Auld Lang Syne' the perfect song for marking such occasions as the end of the old year and the start of the new. It is both a celebration of friendship, present and continuing, as well as a look back to times that are past.

It says something profound about Life, specifically our relationship to Time. We look back nostalgically at happy times in the past, as we are pulled forward into the future. Change is inevitable and nothing lasts forever. The song is a poignant reminder of this, of our own mortality, and that friendship is the most important thing and should be celebrated.

On a personal note, this was brought home to me earlier this year. I found out that Ross Laird, my best friend from childhood, had died, aged 61. We were inseparable from the ages of 5 to 15 and then drifted apart and lost touch. He was the very best of friends and we shared many childhood adventures together: going to football matches, the Edinburgh Military Tattoo, Judo lessons, mountain climbing, bike rides, and long summers playing football in the park opposite his house. And just like the verses in 'Auld Lang Syne' we wandered over the hillsides together and paddled in the Figgate Park burn. Over the years I thought often about reconnecting with him but had no obvious and easy way of doing so (I couldn't find him on Facebook!) and kept putting it off, thinking I'd do it when I retired and moved back to Edinburgh. But time didn't wait for me or for Ross. Now it is too late and we'll never sit together again and take a drink for the sake of 'auld lang syne'. The lesson I've learned from this is that friends are the most important thing in life. It was pointless me sitting remembering my childhood in an abstract way, mourning the loss of this toy or that toy. The real jewel from my childhood was the people I spent it with. The people who matter in our lives are irreplaceable and we should be with them and celebrate them **now**. Burns got it. I've only just, at the age of 61, got it.

As children we experience Time as slow and our summer days are so long that we think our childhood will last forever. Burns perfectly captures that experience, bringing it to our attention, and at the same time distancing us with lines like, 'But seas between us braid hae roar'd'. The word roared is especially powerful here, giving us a sense of the power of time and distance over us. It reminds me of Dylan Thomas' elegy to his dying father: 'rage, rage, against the dying of the light'. Perhaps, in the end, all we can do is 'roar' against loss. However, the song is more optimistic than that, Burns is telling us - despite everything, friendship endures. The song ends, as 'John Anderson, my Jo' does, with a positive affirmation. The unity of lovers and friends endures, and even death cannot diminish that.

Chapter 8

TIME AND TIDE
1788 to 1796

'Nae man can tether time or tide'

We left Robert Burns in May 1788 after he made four life-changing decisions:

- To settle down with Jean Armour in matrimonial bliss
- To rent the larger Ellisland farm near Dumfries
- To achieve financial security by taking a lucrative job with the Excise in Dumfries
- To focus on the unpaid work of collecting, editing and writing new Scottish songs for publication in Johnson's **The Scots Musical Museum**.

Exciseman (1788)

Let us rejoin him in 1788 at the age of 29, for the remaining 8 years of his life.

In June a letter from his friend Ainslie told him that Jenny Clow, Nancy's servant, was pregnant.

Burns had moved, alone, into Ellisland to supervise building work being done there to make a suitable home for his family. While Jean remained in Mauchline, Burns spent the rest of the year commuting, on horseback, the 43 miles between the two homes.

In July Burns obtained confirmation of an Excise job, which he began in the late summer. Some biographers report his initial earnings as £35 per annum, and others claim £50. By my calculation (see Appendix 2), the lower figure would be worth at least £52, 500 today and the upper, £75,000 – two times or three times the current national average – proving that Burns' poverty was either self-inflicted or, more probably, mainly psychological. The large area he was allocated (Upper Nithsdale, covering ten parishes) meant he had to ride between 120 and 200 miles a week on horseback over rough terrain, and in all weathers.

Nowadays, sitting in our 'climate controlled' cars with modern suspensions, comfortable adjustable seats, cup holders, radio/mp3 players, headlights, mirrors, built in satellite navigation, power steering and 'cruise control' on smooth, well-marked, well-lit roads and motorways with 'cats' eyes' we never give a thought to roads in the late 18th century. Tarmac was not invented until 1820 and the 'roads' Burns travelled were dirt roads – muddy in winter, hard and dry in summer. Reaching the towns and villages he may have encountered the dubious luxury of cobbles: his knee never fully recovered from its encounter with an Edinburgh cobble. The city of Edinburgh, preserving its history, has many cobbled streets and travelling over them on a bicycle or a car is a bone-rattling experience. I remember getting a new bike and by the time I rode it home half the nuts and bolts had come loose (some had even pinged off onto the road to be lost forever); my groin was red raw; and half my teeth wobbled in their sockets. Okay, I'm exaggerating – but not by much!

Excisemen were every bit as popular as taxmen are today, and also faced the possibility of dangerous encounters with smugglers. So, for self-defence, Burns was required to carry two pistols – the kind you imagine Highwaymen like Dick Turpin to have carried. There is no record that he ever had occasion to use them but they are preserved today in The National Museum of Scotland in Chambers Street, Edinburgh.

Jenny Clow gave birth to a son, Robert (in November 1788) and issued Burns with a writ demanding money for his upkeep. It is believed that Burns travelled to Edinburgh and settled with her for an undisclosed sum. He also offered to take custody, but Jenny decided to keep the boy.

Revolution and Tam (1789 to 1790)

In the Spring of 1789 the building work at Ellisland farm was finally completed and Jean moved in.

Domestic stability for Burns coincided with turbulent times elsewhere.

In France, the people had become tired of being poor and starving while the aristocracy lived in opulent palaces surrounded by servants and treasure, completely out of touch with the plight of their subjects. There is the famous but probably apocryphal story of Marie Antoinette, the wife of Louis XVI, who, on being told that the peasants were starving because they had no bread to eat, looked bewildered and said, 'Let them eat cake!'

On 14th July 1789 the Paris Bastille was stormed, sending a ripple of fear around the Royal Courts, stately homes, and parliaments of Europe. The Bastille, traditionally a prison for political prisoners, was a symbol of monarchy and tyranny. It also housed a large store of gunpowder and arms which were now seized. Symbolically, and practically, this was a significant victory for the revolutionaries and signalled that The French Revolution had begun in earnest. Liberal democracy was on its way.

On 18th August 1789 Jean gave birth to another son, Francis Wallace Burns.

In September Burns began a new Excise role in Dumfries: allocated a smaller territory he was now able to work on foot, spared the exhausting days in the saddle.

This year, somehow, Burns found the time and energy to write new songs. He contributed to two editions of **The Scots Musical Museum** and the third edition came out in 1790, featuring additional Burns' lyrics, including: 'John, Anderson my Jo'; 'My Heart's in the Highlands'; and several Jacobite songs (a clear indicator where his political sympathies lay).

In July 1790, Burns was promoted to the Dumfries Third Foot-Walk and a salary of £70 per annum (equivalent to at least £105,000 today).

Also, in 1790, Burns wrote his comic masterpiece, 'Tam o' Shanter'. It is easy to see where he got his inspiration. As a child his imagination had been sparked by a relative, Betty Davidson, who lived with the family at Lochlea. She had, according to Burns, an inexhaustible supply of stories of ghoulies, ghosties, warlocks and witches.

Like the eponymous hero of his poem, Burns would, on more than one occasion, have a tipple after work in the local hostelry, The Globe Inn. Then, slightly inebriated he would jump on his horse and ride the six and a half miles from Dumfries to Ellisland farm. In the dark, and the wind, and the rain, the old stories of Betty would combine with the alcohol and the rhythmic, hypnotic gait of the horse. Who knows what phantoms he imagined on wild, stormy nights as he rode alone?

'Tam o' Shanter' is a rollicking good read. I include it in full here.

Spoiler alert: the basic story is that Tam o' Shanter is riding home at Halloween, a little worse for wear, and he happens upon a witches' coven at a local church. He spies upon them as they disrobe, is discovered, and flees. He is chased all the way to the River Doon and is nearly caught. As Tam's horse crosses the middle of the river a witch grabs his horse's tail, and it rips off, allowing rider and horse a narrow escape (witches cannot cross running water).

Tam o' Shanter

When **chapman billies** leave the street, [peddlar friends]
And **drouthy neibors**, neibors, meet; [drunken neighbours]
As market days are wearing late,
And folk begin to tak the gate,
While we sit **bousing** at the nappy,   [boozing]
An' getting **fou** and **unco** happy,   [full=drunk][uncommonly]
We think na on the lang Scots miles,
The mosses, waters, **slaps** and stiles,   [gaps in fences]
That lie between us and our **hame**,   [home]
Where sits our **sulky, sullen dame**,   [the wife!]

Time and Tide

Gathering her brows like gathering storm,
Nursing her wrath to keep it warm.

This truth fand honest Tam o' Shanter,
As he frae Ayr ae night did canter:
(Auld Ayr, **wham** ne'er a town surpasses,   [whom]
For honest men and bonie lasses).

O Tam! had'st thou but been sae wise,
As **taen** thy ain wife Kate's advice!   [taken]
She tauld thee weel thou was a **skellum**,   [scoundrel]
A blethering, blustering, drunken **blellum**;   [blusterer]
That frae November till October,
Ae market-day thou was na sober;
That **ilka melder** wi' the Miller,   [every last milling]
Thou sat as lang as thou had siller;   [silver = money]
That ev'ry **naig** was ca'd a shoe on   [small horse]
The Smith and thee gat roarin' fou on;
That at the Lord's house, ev'n on Sunday,
Thou drank wi' Kirkton Jean till Monday,
She prophesied that late or soon,
Thou wad be found, deep drown'd in Doon,
Or catch'd wi' warlocks in the **mirk**,   [dark]
By Alloway's auld, haunted **kirk**.   [church]

Ah, gentle dames! it **gars me greet**,   [makes me cry]
To think how mony counsels sweet,
How mony lengthen'd, sage advices,
The husband frae the wife despises!

But to our tale: Ae market night,
Tam had got planted unco right,
Fast by an **ingle, bleezing** finely,   [blazing fire]
Wi **reaming swats**, that drank divinely;   [foaming ales]
And at his elbow, Souter Johnie,
His ancient, trusty, droughty crony:
Tam lo'ed him like a very brither;

They had been **fou** for weeks thegither.

The night drave on wi' sangs an' **clatter**;　　[gossip]
And aye the ale was growing better:
The Landlady and Tam grew **gracious**,　　[friendly]
Wi' favours secret, sweet, and precious:
The Souter tauld his queerest stories;
The Landlord's laugh was ready chorus:
The storm without might **rair** and rustle,　　[roar]
Tam did na mind the storm a whistle.

Care, mad to see a man sae happy,
E'en drown'd himsel amang the **nappy**.　　[ale]
As bees flee hame wi' lades o' treasure,
The minutes wing'd their way wi' pleasure:
Kings may be blest, but Tam was glorious,
O'er a' the ills o' life victorious!

But pleasures are like poppies spread,
You seize the flow'r, its bloom is shed;
Or like the snow falls in the river,
A moment white - then melts for ever;
Or like the Borealis race,
That flit ere you can point their place;
Or like the Rainbow's lovely form
Evanishing amid the storm. -
Nae man can tether Time nor Tide,
The hour approaches Tam **maun** ride;　　[must]
That hour, o' night's black arch the key-stane,
That dreary hour he mounts his beast in;
And **sic** a night he taks the road in,　　[such]
As ne'er poor sinner was abroad in.
The wind blew as 'twad blawn its last;
The rattling showers rose on the blast;
The speedy gleams the darkness swallow'd;
Loud, deep, and lang, the thunder bellow'd:
That night, a child might understand,
The **deil** had business on his hand.　　[devil]

Weel-mounted on his grey mare, Meg,
A better never lifted leg,

Tam **skelpit** on thro' **dub** and mire,   [hurried] [puddle]
Despising wind, and rain, and fire;
Whiles holding fast his gude blue bonnet,
Whiles crooning o'er some auld Scots sonnet,
Whiles **glow'rin** round wi' prudent cares,   [staring]
Lest **bogles** catch him unawares;   [ghosts, spirits]
Kirk-Alloway was drawing nigh,
Where **ghaists and houlets** nightly cry.   [ghosts and owls]

By this time he was cross the ford,
Where in the **snaw** the chapman **smoor'd**; [snow, smothered]
And past the **birks** and **meikle stane**,   [birch; giant stone]
Where drunken Charlie **brak's neck-bane**; [broke his neck]
And thro' the **whins**, and by the cairn,   [gorse]
Where hunters fand the murder'd bairn;
And near the thorn, **aboon** the well,   [above]
Where Mungo's mither hang'd hersel'.
Before him Doon pours all his floods,
The doubling storm roars thro' the woods,
The lightnings flash from pole to pole,
Near and more near the thunders roll,
When, glimmering thro' the groaning trees,
Kirk-Alloway seem'd in a bleeze,
Thro' ilka bore the beams were glancing,
And loud resounded mirth and dancing.

Inspiring bold **John Barleycorn**!   [alcohol]
What dangers thou canst make us scorn!
Wi' **tippenny**, we fear nae evil;   [two penny]
Wi' **usquabae**, we'll face the devil!   [whisky]
The swats sae ream'd in Tammie's **noddle**, [brain]
Fair play, he car'd na deils a **boddle**,   [farthing, a coin]
But Maggie stood, **right sair** astonish'd,   [right sore = greatly]
Till, by the heel and hand admonish'd,
She ventur'd forward on the light;
And, wow! Tam saw an unco sight!

Warlocks and witches in a dance:
Nae **cotillon**, **brent** new frae France, [a French dance; brand]

But hornpipes, jigs, strathspeys, and reels,
Put life and **mettle** in their heels. [spirit]
A **winnock-bunker** in the east, [window seat]
There sat auld Nick, in shape o' beast;
A **towzie tyke**, black, grim, and large, [shaggy dog]
To gie them music was his charge:
He screw'd the pipes and **gart them skirl**, [made them squeal]
Till roof and rafters a' did **dirl**. - [ring]
Coffins stood round, like open **presses**, [cupboards]
That shaw'd the Dead in their last dresses;
And (by some devilish **cantraip sleight**) [magic trick]
Each in its cauld hand held a light.
By which heroic Tam was able
To note upon the **haly** table, [holy]
A murderer's **banes**, in **gibbet-airns**; [bones; iron cage for displaying criminals]
Twa **span-lang**, wee, unchristened bairns;
A thief, new-cutted frae a **rape**, [rope]
Wi' his last gasp his gab did gape;
Five tomahawks, wi' blude red-rusted:
Five scimitars, wi' murder crusted;
A garter which a babe had strangled:
A knife, a father's throat had mangled.
Whom his ain son of life bereft,
The grey-hairs yet stack to the heft;
Wi' mair of horrible and awfu',
Which even to name wad be unlawfu'.
Three lawyers tongues, turned inside oot,
Wi' lies, seamed like a beggars clout,
Three priests hearts, rotten, black as muck,
Lay stinkin, vile in every **neuk**. [corner]
As Tammie glowr'd, amaz'd, and curious,
The mirth and fun grew fast and furious;
The Piper loud and louder blew,
The dancers quick and quicker flew,
They reel'd, they set, they cross'd, they **cleekit**, [linked arms]
Till **ilka carlin swat and reekit**, [every witch sweated and stank]

And **coost her duddies** to the **wark**, [cast off her ragged clothes; floor]
And **linkit** at it in her **sark**! [danced around; underskirt, petticoat]

Now Tam, O Tam! had they been **queans**, [young girls]
A' plump and strapping in their teens!
Their sarks, instead o' **creeshie flainen**, [greasy flannel]
Been snaw-white seventeen hunder linen!-
Thir breeks o' mine, my only pair, [these trousers]
That ance were plush o' guid blue hair,
I wad hae gien them off my **hurdies**, [buttocks]
For ae blink o' the **bonie burdies**! [pretty maidens]
But wither'd **beldams**, auld and droll, [old women]
Rigwoodie hags wad **spean a foal**, [gnarled; put a foal off its food]
Louping an' flinging on a **crummock**. [leaping; stick]
I wonder did na turn thy stomach.

But Tam **kent** what was what fu' **brawlie**: [knew; very well]
There was ae winsome wench and **waulie** [handsome]
That night enlisted in the core,
Lang after ken'd on Carrick shore;
(For many a beast to dead she shot,
And perish'd mony a bonie boat,
And shook baith meikle corn and bear,
And kept the country-side in fear);
Her **cutty sark**, o' **Paisley harn**, [short underskirt; course cloth made in Paisley]
That while a lassie she had worn,
In longitude tho' sorely scanty,
It was her best, and she was **vauntie**. [proud]
Ah! little ken'd thy reverend **grannie**, [granny]
That sark she **coft** for her wee Nannie, [bought]
Wi twa pund Scots ('twas a' her riches),
Wad ever grac'd a dance of witches!

But here my Muse her wing maun **cour**, [drop]
Sic flights are far beyond her power;

To sing how Nannie **lap and flang**,   [leaped and kicked]
(A **souple jade** she was and strang),   [supple lass]
And how Tam stood, like ane bewithc'd,
And thought his very **een** enrich'd: [eyes]
Even Satan glowr'd, and **fidg'd fu' fain**, [moved excitedly]
And **hotch'd** and blew wi' might and **main**: [jerked; strength]
Till first ae **caper**, syne anither,   [caper]
Tam **tint** his reason a thegither,   [lost]
And roars out, 'Weel done, Cutty-sark!'
And in an instant all was dark:
And scarcely had he Maggie rallied.
When out the hellish legion sallied.

As bees bizz out wi' angry fyke,
When plundering herds assail their **byke**;   [hive]
As open **pussie's** mortal foes,   [hare's]
When, pop! she starts before their nose;
As eager runs the market-crowd,
When 'Catch the thief!' resounds aloud;
So Maggie runs, the witches follow,
Wi' mony an **eldritch** skreich and hollow.   [unearthly]

Ah, Tam! Ah, Tam! thou'll get thy **fairin**!   [reward]
In hell, they'll roast thee like a herrin!
In vain thy Kate awaits thy comin!
Kate soon will be a woefu' woman!
Now, do thy speedy-utmost, Meg,
And win the key-stone o' the brig;
There, at them thou thy tail may toss,
A running stream they dare na cross.
But ere the keystane she could make,
The **fient** a tail she had to shake!   [fiend]
For Nannie, far before the rest,
Hard upon noble Maggie **prest**,   [chased]
And flew at Tam wi' furious **ettle**;   [aim]
But little **wist** she Maggie's mettle!   [was]
Ae spring brought off her master **hale**,   [whole]
But left behind her ain grey tail:
The **carlin claught** her by the rump,   [witch; clutched]

And left poor Maggie scarce a stump.

Now, wha this tale o' truth shall read,
Ilk man and mother's son, take heed:
Whene'er to Drink you are inclin'd,
Or Cutty-sarks rin in your mind,
Think ye may buy the joys o'er dear;
Remember Tam o' Shanter's mare.

In addition to the familiarity of the trip, and the experience of horseriding, slightly inebriated, alone in the dark, there is an extra hint of autobiography here: just like Tam, Robert Burns was getting 'friendly' with the barmaid. After a day's work at the Excise, rather than travel home to Ellisland, Burns often stayed overnight in Dumfries at The Globe Inn, with his new mistress, twenty one year old Ann Park.

The sexual content of the poem and the warning at the end to avoid being tempted by women in 'cutty – sarks' (short skirts) helps us see the loss of the tail as a symbolic castration. Perhaps Burns was feeling anxious about the consequences of his affair with Ann Park, or perhaps he was just adding a conventional 'moral' to round off the story with a smile?

Dumfries (1791)

In March 1791, Ann Park bore Robert a daughter, Elizabeth (Betty).

Soon after, on 9th April, Jean bore him a son, William Nicol.

Ellisland farm was proving to be no more successful than all the previous Burns' farming ventures, draining his time, energy and money. In a letter to Gilbert he described it as 'a ruinous affair on all hands' (Crawford, p.320). So, with the Excise job going well, Burns gave up the lease on 10th September and moved his growing family to a house in the Wee Vennel (now known as 11 Bank Street), Dumfries.

On 27th December Burns joined St. Andrew's Masonic Lodge in Dumfries.

Smugglers (1792)

Jenny Clow died of tuberculosis in January. The fate of her child, Robert, is unknown. Burns had offered to take in the child when Jenny was alive, but there is no record of him ever seeing his son again after her death. Some accounts suggest young Robert went on to prosper in London, but others suggest he died young, probably soon before or soon after his mother Jenny.

On 29th January Nancy McLehose, who by now had realised the limitations of her love affair with Burns, sailed for Jamaica intending to reconcile with her estranged husband, giving Burns instruction not to write to her while she was there. She and Burns were to correspond after but were never to meet again.

Before Nancy left Burns sent her, 'Ae Fond Kiss'. It is difficult to read without reaching the conclusion that there is more than artifice here; the lyric is an expression of the most searing pain, and I have no doubt that Burns felt it deeply. He was a complex man, capable of profound sensitivity and emotion – the only question is how long and how consistently he felt these emotions. I am reminded of his own admission, 'My heart is tinder'. Such volatility and intensity cannot be sustained, but there is no doubt that it was part of Burns' psychological makeup. Without it, he would not have been the poet he was. If we judge him harshly for his moral shortcomings we must also remember that he also displayed a sense of loyalty and honour, stood by his family, his friends, his women and his children, and forgave others their foibles and shortcomings. The only exceptions were those that attacked him; and even then he found revenge in satire: e.g. mocking religious hypocrisy in 'Holy Willie's Prayer'.

In April 1792 Burns was promoted to the Dumfries Port Division of the Excise.

Crawford (p. 348) states that Burns' earnings, which were already £70 p.a. were boosted by an additional £20 (which, by my reckoning – explained in Appendix 2 – would give him a salary worth at least £135,000 in 2020). However, other sources suggest that his top salary with the Excise was £70 per annum, not counting bonuses.

There is a story relating to this new role: Burns, brandishing a sword (or perhaps his 'Dick Turpin' pistols?), led the charge on a smuggling schooner, grounded on mud flats in the Solway Firth. He was already a reliable and diligent tax collector, and the story adds the gloss of heroism. Happily, the smugglers abandoned ship and fled – there is no more terrifying sight than an armed Romantic poet running towards you - and no one was shot.

One perk of the Excise job was that a share of the contraband went to the Excisemen who collected it, which prompted another story about Burns, that he sent one of the canons they found aboard the smugglers' ship to the revolutionaries in France to aid them in their cause. If true this would probably have resulted in Burns being charged with treason. The story has never been supported by evidence, and is most likely false.

In the evenings Burns continued to work on his lyrical art and, in the late summer of 1792, he sent 13 songs to Johnson for the 4th volume of **The Scots Musical Museum**. Two thirds of the songs in this edition are by Burns, including, 'The Bonnie Banks o'Doon' (see chapter 4) and 'A Parcel o'Rogues' (see chapter 6). He did not sign his name to the latter because, as a government officer, voicing political views was strictly not allowed and potentially dangerous for his career and his health.

Also, Burns was asked by George Thomson (an Edinburgh lawyer and keen amateur musician) to contribute songs to a new publication, an upmarket music book called, **A Select Collection of Original Scottish Airs**, and to name his price.

Burns was delighted to contribute, but declined any payment. He saw poetry as a pure endeavour not to be sullied with money. He took offence and in a letter offered his services free stating that accepting payment would be 'sodomy of the soul'. His first biographer, Currie, a prudish, reformed alcoholic, changed that to 'prostitution of the soul' to spare the sensibilities of the public.

Thomas Paine's scandalous book **The Rights of Man**, published the year before, had been a best-seller. But the Establishment took a very dim view of people who stirred up the peasants with foolish notions of equality, democracy, healthcare, and pensions and decided to try him for *seditious libel*.

Assuming, rightly, that the result of the trial was a foregone conclusion – a guilty verdict carrying a possible life sentence - Paine fled to revolutionary France, where he could find more sympathy for his ideas. In his absence, he was found guilty and the court case set a precedent for the government to charge others for having the 'wrong views'.

Burns was privately sympathetic to Paine, but as a government employee could not express his views openly.

Domestically, the year 1792 ended on a sour and a happy note. Ann Park's fate is unknown but there is some evidence that she died soon after giving birth to Burns' daughter Betty in Leith. At some point this year (or possibly the year before) Jean welcomed the orphaned Betty into the family home and raised her as her own. Then, on 21st November, Jean bore Burns another daughter, Elizabeth Riddell Burns.

Radical (1793 to 1794)

The French Revolution was hotting up. On 21st January 1793 Louis XVI was guillotined and on 1st February France declared war on Britain. The war was to last from 1793 to 1802.

How did Burns feel about the French Revolution?

Burns was capable of verbal pyrotechnics and flamboyant theatrics and, as his poems and songs show, had a natural love of his fellow man and a sense of egalitarian brotherhood. However, he was a man of feeling rather than intellect, and it is doubtful that he had a coherent, consistent political philosophy. Rather, he had a sense of his own intellectual superiority, and a chip on his shoulder because the upper class, lacking his gifts and intellect, outranked him in wealth and status. Occasionally, he expressed as much, whether through satirical verse, letters, or public speaking - and this got him in hot water. As a servant of the Excise, he was forbidden to express any political views – never mind revolutionary ones – and had faced a few serious investigations where his conduct was called into question. On one occasion it was regarding a submission he made to a radical journal. On another occasion, on 26th November 1792, there was a controversy about his not removing his hat in the Dumfries theatre when 'God Save the King' was sung - hardly a radical act by today's un-deferential standards, but enough in the 1790's to land him in potentially serious trouble. Notable people had been tried for less, found guilty, and been imprisoned or exiled to the colonies.

Luckily, Burns had enough influential patrons to deflect any serious charges and, after an informal dressing down following an inquiry by his employers into his political conduct, he not only kept his job with the Excise but was soon promoted.

Leading a political double-life, Burns publically showed his support for the King, but privately voiced his republican sympathies. In one letter of 1793, Burns gives his frank opinion of politics: 'a science wherewith, by means of nefarious cunning, & hypocritical pretence, we govern civil polities for the emolument of ourselves & our adherents.'

That has certainly been the case in British politics over my lifetime. Aristophanes got it right when he said, 'Look under a rock, and you'll find a politician.'

In 1793 Nancy returned from Jamaica. Her attempt to rekindle her marriage floundered when she found her husband had an 'ebony mistress and mahogany children' (McIntyre, p.339).

Burns wrote to her, keen to resume their correspondence, and they did to a limited extent, but their romance was over. Some biographers have suggested that she took up with Burns' friend Ainslie (the rogue), which, if true, strikes me as a sour, ignominious end to one of the world's great love stories.

In March 1793, Burns asked for and was made a 'Freeman' of Dumfries. One main benefit of this was free schooling for his children.

In May, he moved his family into a larger, two-storey house in Dumfries, 24 Mill Hole Brae. Today it is a museum and the street has been renamed, Burns Street.

Burns toured Galloway in July 1793. Thomson sent him 100 airs, requesting verses, and Burns obliged with two of his finest and most famous lyrics, 'My Luve is Like a Red, Red Rose' and 'Scots Wha Hae'. The first edition of Thomson's **A Select Collection of Original Scottish Airs** was published, including 'My Luve is Like a Red, Red Rose' and 'A Man's a Man for a' That / Is There for Honest Poverty'.

Many biographers exaggerate Burns' money worries but around this time he turned down an invitation from a London newspaper to write a column. He was offered 1 guinea (£1.05) a week, equivalent to at least £75,000 a year in today's money). So, it is hard to take Burns' protestations of poverty too seriously.

Burns was also in great demand socially and a regular guest at various aristocratic homes. Home life with Jean (homely, forgiving and sensual Jean), although harmonious, did not give him the intellectual stimulus he needed. He exchanged many letters with an older widow, Mrs. Dunlop, to whom he sent his poems and lyrics for critique, she taking on the role of a mentor. He also became friendly with the Riddells, especially the young, intelligent, literary Maria Riddell. Their friendship soured briefly (all was forgiven the following year) after he committed some social faux pas with her sister. Carswell (p.356) presents it as a drunken male game that went too far with, perhaps, an element of the aristocratic men setting up the lower class poet (ibid). Otherwise, there is not the slightest hint of impropriety regarding these female friendships and it seems that Burns was faithful (at least physically) to Jean for the rest of his life.

Burns was still prone to infatuations and found a new muse – seventeen year old, Jean Lorimer. It is doubtful there was ever a physical component to their relationship but Burns did write some emotionally charged poems dedicated to her.

On 12th August 1794, the other Jean, the one he was married to, gave birth to James Glencairn Burns.

In December, Burns was promoted to Acting Supervisor of Excise, in order to cover for his boss, Findlater, who was off ill for several months.

The Awkward Squad (1795)

The Excise deputising role once again entailed long journeys on horseback, in a particularly bad winter of heavy snowfall. Burns was keen to show the Excise that he was reliable, loyal, and worthy of further promotion after doubts had been raised previously over his politics. He had his eye on promotion, knowing that only a few ranks higher the financial reward was exceedingly high and the workload much less. However, covering for Findlater took a toll on his already deteriorating health.

Meanwhile, the war with France was going badly for the British. There were food shortages and a growing feeling that invasion was likely.

In an abstract sense Burns may have supported the ideals of the Revolution, but in a practical way, he didn't support French revolutionaries invading Britain.

He attended a meeting in January to set up a local Dumfries Volunteer Corps and officially joined the Corps on 21st February 1795. As a government employee he was expected to. This was a kind of Home Guard, or 'Dad's Army', but it was taken very seriously, even by Burns - despite him humorously dubbing it, 'The Awkward Squad'. Burns had a perfect attendance record and gave exemplary service. The Corps observed strict discipline and met frequently for target practice, and for drills (performed in front of an approving public audience).

Infamously, the bill for the uniform was to be paid by individual members and stood at an eye-watering cost of £8 7s (more than a farm labourer's annual wage - an equivalent of £12,000+ in today's money). The excessively fine uniform would have been chosen by the rich, aristocrats commanding the unit and this would have been a relatively paltry sum to them. It is small wonder that Burns balked at paying it and delayed.

Burns political double-life continued. On one hand he was privately expressing republican, pro-revolutionary sentiments: 'A Man's a Man for a' That' was published anonymously in a Glasgow magazine. But, publicly, he was a loyalist, although his public expressions of support for the King always contained some playful ambiguity – ambiguous enough for plausible denial:

> Who, will not sing, GOD SAVE THE KING,
> Shall hang as high's the steeple;
> But while we sing, GOD SAVE THE KING,
> We'll ne'er forget THE PEOPLE!
> Fal de ral &c.
>
> (Crawford, p.385)

Domestically, the year was to end badly. Burns' and Jean's daughter, Elizabeth Riddell Burns died, aged four, in September.

Burns was too ill to attend the funeral, and suffered acute 'hypochondria' (depression) for the remainder of the year, taking to his 'sick bed' from December through to January.

Flying Gout (1796)

Dumfries was struggling with famine brought on by the war with France. In March, troops were in the streets to quell food riots and there were curbs on freedom of speech and assembly. There are parallels with the situation developing in Britain (and elsewhere) at the moment with the Covid 19 virus threatening food shortages, the Scottish government attempting to pass a bill that will outlaw 'hate speech' (even in the privacy of one's own home), and the country once again under 'Lockdown', after a long spell where gatherings have been restricted to six people.

At home, Jean was pregnant again.

Burns health improved, but by the late spring he was in a final, rapid decline.

Doctor William Maxwell diagnosed 'flying gout' (a type of moving arthritis) and recommended a daily regime of energetic horse riding and bathing in the Solway Firth (to enjoy the invigorating delights of the Atlantic Ocean). Burns followed this insane advice and went to a small place called Brow some ten miles from Dumfries to engage in the daily torture which, rather than cure him, probably greatly accelerated his demise.

During this period he couldn't work and his salary was halved (but still a respectable £35 p.a.) and he wrote letters to various friends asking for money, and calling in debts. This has been taken as evidence of poverty, but it is more probable that Burns, in his sickness, was worried for his family, and reliving money anxieties from his childhood, especially on Lochlea farm, where his father had been forced to be frugal and the family subsisted for a while on a very basic diet.

Burns took time out from his treatment, to visit Maria Riddell. He greeted her with, 'Well, madam, have you any commands for the other world?' (McIntyre p.402). She was shocked at his emaciated appearance. He knew he was dying but was still capable of making a theatrical entrance and lighting the darkness with gallows humour.

Realising the Doctor's 'cure' wasn't working, Burns returned home to die. He was nursed by Jessy Lewars, an eighteen year old girl, whom he fell in love with and wrote a lyric for, which ends:

> Or were I monarch o'the globe,
> Wi' thee to reign, wi' thee to reign;
> The brightest jewel in my crown,
> Wad by my queen, wad be my queen.
> (McIntyre p. 399)

I have often wondered what his wife Jean thought of all this. Many biographers leave us with the impression that she was an illiterate country bumpkin (and something of a 'doormat' for her philandering, poet husband). Burns himself made a very unflattering comparison between Jean and the sophisticated, well-read Nancy which further gives the impression that Jean was not his ideal wife. However, Crawford (p.179) suggests that Jean was 'remarkable' and quotes a journalist, John McDiarmid, who knew her and described her as: ' 'well-balanced... a clever woman' who 'possessed great shrewdness, discriminated character admirably, and frequently made very pithy remarks'.' (ibid.).

It is difficult, if not impossible, to understand the mechanics of any marriage but, it appears, that Jean was a fine looking, intelligent woman, who could read and write, satisfied Burns physically, and had a capacity for kindness, forgiveness, generosity and understanding that would put the best of us to shame. By all accounts, Burns treated her with respect, cared for her, and valued her. How he and she negotiated his infidelities remains a private matter.

When Burns was close to death, he is alleged to have said to his friend John Gibson, referring to the Dumfries Volunteer Corps, 'John, don't let the awkward squad fire over me.'

He slipped into a delirium and died at 5am on July 21st 1796.

His funeral was a national event. His brother Gilbert was there but Jean Armour couldn't attend as she was giving birth to her 9th and last child, Maxwell.

Burns was buried with due pomp and ceremony in St. Michael's Kirk, Dumfries. Contrary to his wishes, 'The Awkward Squad', did indeed salute him with their guns, firing three volleys over his grave. I think he would have been secretly pleased.

The only bill he left unpaid was for his uniform, but that was soon covered as money kept rolling in from benefactors to ensure that the family of Scotland's best loved poet was financially secure for the rest of their lives.

Chapter 9

The Deil's Awa' Wi' Th' Exciseman

'If there's another world, he lives in bliss;
If there is none, he made the best of this.'
(a mock epitaph Burns wrote for a friend)

To this day we do not know what Burns died of.

One theory is that he died of rheumatic fever.

Another plausible theory was put forward by surgeon Sir James Crichton-Browne who diagnosed, in 1926, that Burns died of **endocarditis**, a disease that causes inflammation of the heart (Grimble, p. 20). He further suggested that the root of this disease was the strain placed on Burns' heart between the ages of 13 and 15, by hard farm labouring on his father's farm while, owing to the family's poverty, being fed an inadequate diet. Grimble (ibid.) concludes, 'In his determination to be a tenant farmer like his fathers before him, William Burness killed Scotland's greatest poet in his prime.'

Alternatively, according to Mackie (Chapter 11) the cause of Burns' death may have been a relatively rare disease called **brucellosis** that can be caught from a variety of farm animals - the symptoms are similar to tuberculosis and rheumatic fever. This theory is also suggested in McIntyre's book (p. 443) and is based on the work of medical experts who concluded that nothing can be proven until the poet's body is examined using modern medical technology.

So far, the relevant authorities have refused to allow Burns' remains to be exhumed for medical examination and the cause of his death remains a question for posterity to answer.

Burns may have died at the age of 37, but he 'made the best of this [world]' in a short, but eventful life.

He was a complex character. Even in an age when life expectancy was low, Burns had more than his fair share of heartache, losing a father, brothers, lovers and children to early deaths. Sometimes he worried and despaired, succumbing to his 'hypochondria', but he was mostly full of humour, mischief and fun. His emotional highs and lows were channelled into poetry, song, letters, and essays. His range was remarkable, from tender love songs to cutting satires on politics and religion.

Above all, Burns was determined to be Scotland's Bard: to know the people and its folksong, and to make a lasting record of its culture. He lived at a certain point in the history of two kingdoms, Scotland and England, and his life and ideas were affected by their political and religious conflicts and uneasy union. With his art he captured and preserved the soul of Scotland, when it was in danger of being anglicised out of existence.

His childhood hero was William Wallace and Burns was, at heart, a Jacobite and a patriot. On his visit to Bannockburn, he used a diamond stylus to engrave seditious verse on a window in a Stirling Inn. Realising it could, and definitely would, have led to serious trouble, he returned and broke the window. This could be interpreted as cowardice, but to leave the evidence there would have been self-destructive folly. Here is the verse:

> Here Stewarts once in triumph reign'd,
> And laws for Scotland's weal ordain'd;
> Bur now unroof'd their Palace stands,
> Their Sceptre's fall'n to other hands;
> Fall'n indeed unto the Earth
> Whence grovelling reptiles take their birth;
> And since great Stewarts' line is gone,
> A race outlandish fills their throne;
> An idiot race to honour lost,
> Who know them best dispise them most.

Burns often let his heart, his emotions, lead his intellect and his reason, but calling the current King's lineage an 'idiot race to honour lost' would have resulted, at the very least, in dismissal from his government post with the Excise, and dishonour and poverty for his growing number of dependents.

Burns was also the first of the Romantic poets, writing about feelings and Nature using the language of the ordinary people. His republican sympathies, his championing of the common man, his egalitarianism, and his distaste for the hypocrisy of Church and State, were radical and dangerous in his lifetime but still found expression in his songs, influencing and shaping the ideas that led to the free, democratic societies we enjoy in the West today. Burns is still loved, still relevant, because he helped create **our** zeitgeist. Many of us think like Burns and the Romantics thought: we believe in equality, free speech, and the 'pursuit of Happiness', even if we sometimes disagree on the best way to achieve these things.

He was a sociable man and an eloquent public speaker. Personal accounts by people who knew him all agree that his poetry was brilliant, but his conversation was even more impressive.

He also had eyes that blazed!

In Edinburgh, Walter Scott, only fifteen years old, met Burns at a social gathering and reported that his eyes, 'glowed, I say literally glowed' (Grimble, p.108).

His good friend, Maria Riddell described him thus:

His features were stamped with the hardy character of independence, and the firmness of conscious, though not arrogant, pre-eminence; the animated expressions of countenance were almost peculiar to himself; the rapid lightnings of his eye were always the harbinger of some flash of genius, whether they darted the fiery glances of insulted and indignant superiority, or beamed with the impassioned sentiment of fervent and impetuous affections affections. His voice alone could improve upon the magic of his eye; sonorous, replete with the finest modulations, it alternately captivated the ear with the melody of poetic numbers, the perspicuity of nervous reasoning, or the ardent sallies of enthusiastic patriotism. (Grimble, p.8)

Charismatic, sensitive, patriotic, idealistic, and at times highly irresponsible, Burns will be remembered first and foremost for his poetry and song.

The last word in this book should go to him. The anthem of nostalgic friendship, 'Auld Lang Syne', would be appropriate; as would the ultimate song of parting, 'Ae Fond Kiss'.

However, I think Burns would like to leave us with a dance and a smile.

He loved to poke fun at hypocrites, and always felt a tension between his role as a government employee, swearing allegiance to King George of the 'idiot race', and his true inclinations as an anti-establishment, champion of the common man – a Jacobite sympathiser and a Republican.

This final song (first published in **The Scots Musical Museum** in 1792) is from the perspective of ordinary people, rejoicing that the Exciseman has got his just deserts and been taken by the devil to hell. They celebrate by making their ale, delighted that he is no longer around to tax them for it.

Burns is believed to have written this song soon after the episode of the smugglers in the Solway Firth and then sung it at a social gathering of fellow Excisemen. He turns his wit on his colleagues, but also on himself for his unsuitable choice of profession.

For a man who experienced so much death and loss, Burns can still laugh at his own mortality, and at the devil.

I'd like to end this book by picturing him, defiant to the last, throwing his Excise ledgers to the wind and dancing off into the sunset with Old Nick:

The Deil's Awa' Wi' Th' Exciseman
[the Devil's away with the Exciseman]

The Deil cam fiddlin' through the toun   [the devil came fiddling
And danced awa' wi' th' exciseman,   through the town]
And **ilka** wife cried, **'Auld Mahoun**,   [every; Old Mohammed -
I wish you luck o' the prize, man.'   meaning 'devil']

Chorus:
The Deil's awa,' the Deil's awa',
The Deil's awa' wi' th' Exciseman.
He's danced awa', he's danced awa',
He's danced awa' wl' th' Exciseman.

We'll mak oor **maut** and we'll brew our drink.   [malt, ale]
We'll laugh, sing and rejoice, man,
And **monie braw** thanks to the **miekle** black Deil
That danced awa' wi' th' exciseman.   [**many fine** thanks
                                              to the **great** black Devil]

    Repeat Chorus

There's threesome **reels**; there's foursome **reels**
There's **hornpipes** and **strathspeys**, man,   [traditional dances]
But the **ae** best dance that cam o'er our land   [one]
Was 'The Deil's Awa' Wi' Th' Exciseman'.

    Repeat Chorus

The Deil's awa,' the Deil's awa',
The Deil's awa' wi' th' Exciseman.
He's danced awa', he's danced awa',
He's danced awa' wl' th' Exciseman.

- END-

THE SONGS

ARRANGED FOR GUITAR

Note

The songs are presented in the order they appear in the book.

The arrangements are all for standard tuning: EADGBE. Further, they can be played with a plectrum (flatpicking style) - although there is nothing to stop fingerpickers using their right hand fingers if they prefer.

Many of the arrangements are in the key of D major, which is the most popular key in folk music. For that reason I hope the chord melody arrangements have a utility and value beyond the scope of this book: i.e. the guitarist will become familiar with the recurring chords and scale patterns in D major, some of which are harmonized in thirds. These patterns can then be used in other songs to make fresh arrangements or improvise.

I perform the chord melody arrangements of all 12 songs on **YouTube** and some performances are followed up with a tutorial. The videos can be accessed through this link:

https://www.youtube.com/playlist?list=PLzqwFChU0wVnYgFHgNZJJDtnD2aa7doD4

Alternatively, open **YouTube**. In the Search Box, type, **'ukulele beginner to brilliant'** (the name of my channel). Open my channel. Open the Playlists. Select the Playlist, **'BURNS – GUITAR EDITION'**. **Subscribe** and feel free to ask questions in the Comments Section - I will respond.

Leezie Lindsay (Key D)

Will ye (D) go to the Hielands, Leezie (Bm) Lindsay,
Will ye (D) go to the (D7) Hielands wi' (G) me?
(A) Will ye (D) go to the Hielands, Leezie (Bm) Lindsay,
My (G) pride and my (A) darling to (D) be.

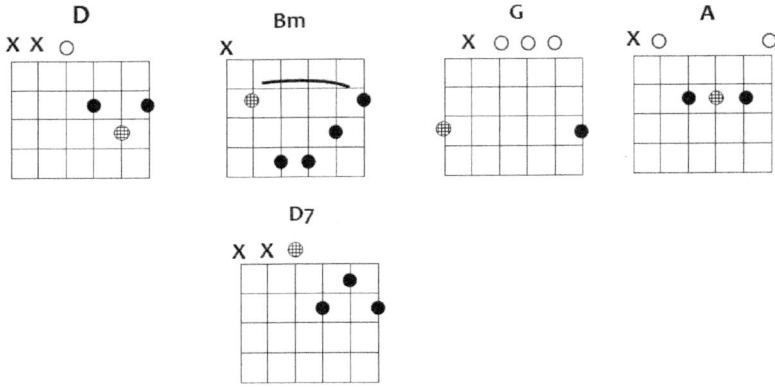

Leezie Lindsay

Leezie Lindsay Chord Melody

John Anderson, my Jo (Key Em)

John (Em) Anderson, my jo, John,
When (D) we were first acquent,
Your (Em) locks were like the raven,
Your (G) bonnie brow was (B7) brent;
But (Em) now your brow is (G) beld, John,
Your (D) locks are like the snaw;
But (Em) blessings (D) on your (Em) frosty pow,
John (Bm) Anderson, my (Em) jo.

John (Em) Anderson, my jo, John,
We (D) clamb the hill thegither;
And (Em) monie a cantie day, John,
We've (G) had wi' ane a- (B7)nither;
Now (Em) we maun totter (G) down, John
And (D) hand in hand we'll go,
And (Em) sleep the (D) gither (Em) at the foot,
John (Bm) Anderson, my (Em) jo.

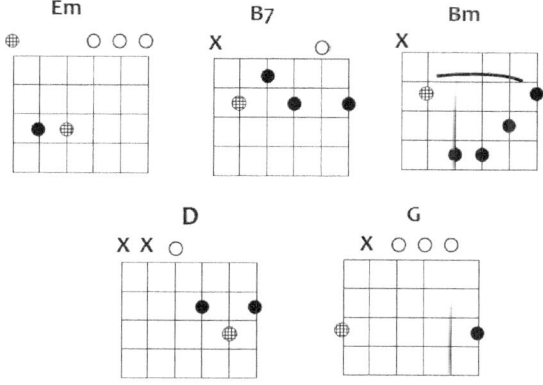

John Anderson, my Jo

John Anderson, my Jo Chord Melody

My Luve is Like a Red, Red Rose (Key G)

O my [G] Luve's like a red, red rose
That's [C] newly sprung in [D] june;
O my [G] Luve's like the melodie
That's [C] sweetly play'd [D] in [G] tune:

As [G] fair art thou, my [C] bonnie [G] lass,
So deep in[C] luve am [D] I:
And [G] I will luve thee [C] still, my [G] dear,
Till a' the [D7] seas gang [G] dry:

Till [G] a' the seas gang dry, my dear,
And [C] the rocks melt wi' the [D] sun:
I will [G] luve thee still, my dear,
While the [C] sands o' life [D] shall [G] run.

And [G] fare thee weel, my [C] only [G] Luve
And fare thee[C] weel, a [D] while!
And [G] I will come a- [C] gain, my [G] Luve,
Tho' it were ten [D7] thousand [G] mile.

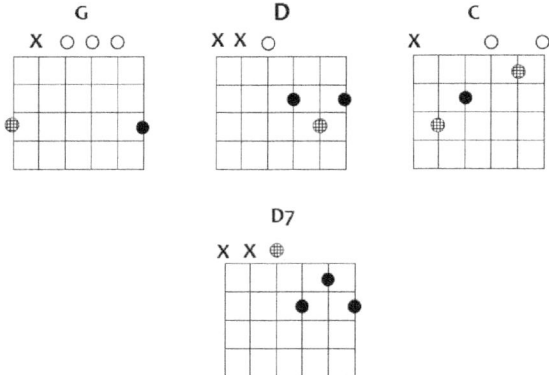

My Luve is Like a Red, Red Rose

My Luve is Like a Red, Red Rose
Chord Melody

Ye Banks and Braes o' Bonnie Doon (Key C)

Ye [C] banks and [Dm] braes o' [C] bonnie [G] Doon,
How [C] can ye [Am] bloom sae [F] fresh and [G] fair;
How [C] can ye [Dm] chant, ye [C] little [G] birds,
And [C] I sae [F] weary, [G] fu' o' [C] care!
Thou'lt [C] break my heart, thou warbling bird,
That wantons thro' the [Am] flowering [G] thorn:
Thou [C] minds me [Dm] o' de- [C] parted [G] joys,
De- [C] parted— [F] never [G] to re- [C] turn!

Aft [C] hae I [Dm] rov'd by [C] bonnie [G] Doon,
To [C] see the [Am] rose and [F] woodbine [G] twine;
And [C] ilka [Dm] bird sang [C] o' its [G] luve,
And [C] fondly [F] sae did [G] I o' [C] mine.
Wi' [C] lightsome heart I pu'd a rose,
Fu' sweet upon its [Am] thorny [G] tree;
And [C] my fause [Dm] luver [C] stole my [G] rose,
But, [C] ah! He [F] left the [G] thorn wi' [C] me.

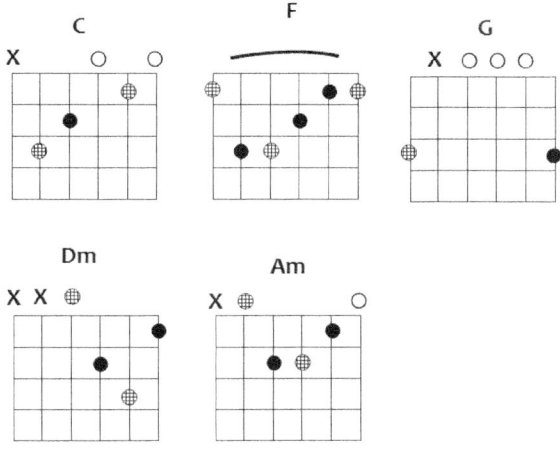

Ye Banks and Braes o' Bonnie Doon

The Songs Arranged for Guitar

Ye Banks and Braes o' Bonnie Doon
Chord Melody

Ye Banks and Braes o' Bonnie Doon (Key G)

Ye [G] banks and [Am] braes o' [G] bonnie [D] Doon,
How [G] can ye [Em] bloom sae [C] fresh and [D] fair;
How [G] can ye [Am] chant, ye [G] little [D] birds,
And [G] I sae [C] weary, [D] fu' o' [G] care!
Thou'lt [G] break my heart, thou warbling bird,
That wantons thro' the [Em] flowering [D] thorn:
Thou [G] minds me [Am] o' de- [G] parted [D] joys,
De- [G] parted- [C] never [D] to re- [G] turn!

Aft [G] hae I [Am] rov'd by [G] bonnie [D] Doon,
To [G] see the [Em] rose and [C] woodbine [D] twine;
And [G] ilka [Am] bird sang [G] o' its [D] luve,
And [G] fondly [C] sae did [D] I o' [G] mine.
Wi' [G] lightsome heart I pu'd a rose,
Fu' sweet upon its [Em] thorny [D] tree;
And [G] my fause [Am] luver [G] stole my [D] rose,
But, [G] ah! He [C] left the [D] thorn wi' [G] me.

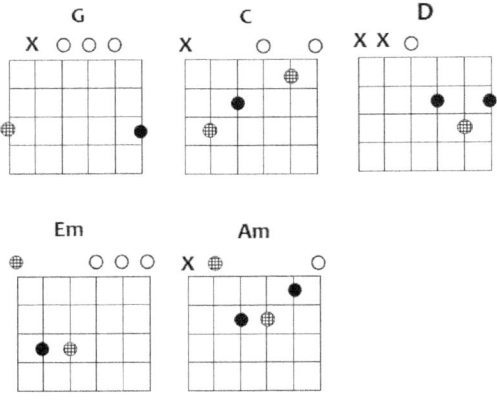

The Songs Arranged for Guitar

Ye Banks and Braes o' Bonnie Doon

Ye Banks and Braes o' Bonnie Doon
Chord Melody

Ae Fond Kiss (Key D)

[D] Ae fond kiss, [G] and [D] then we [Bm] sever;
[G] Ae fareweel, a- [A] las, for [D] ever!
[G] Deep in heart-wrung [D] tears I'll [Bm] pledge thee,
[D] War – [A7] ring [D] sighs [G] and [D] groans I'll [A] wage
[D] thee!

[D] Who shall say [G] that [D] Fortune [Bm] grieves him
[G] While the star of [A] hope she [D] leaves him?
[G] Me, nae cheerfu' [D] twinkle [Bm] lights me,
[D] Dark [A7] des- [D] pair [G] a- [D]round be - [A] nights [D] me.

I'll [D] ne'er blame [G] my [D] partial [Bm] fancy;
[G] Naething could re – [A] sist my [D] Nancy;
[G] But to see her [D] was to [Bm] love her,
[D]Love [A7]but [D] her, [G] and [D] love for [A] e – [D] ver.

[D] Had we ne- [G] ver [D] loved sae [Bm] kindly,
[G] Had we never[A] loved sae [D] blindly,
[G] Never met—or [D] never [Bm] parted,
[D] We [A7] had [D] ne'er [G] been [D] broken- [A] hear – [D] ted.

[D] Fare thee weel, [G] thou [D] first and [Bm] fairest!
[G] Fare thee weel, thou [A] best and [D] dearest!
[G] Thine be ilka [D] joy and [Bm] treasure,
[D] Peace, [A7] en – [D] joy – [G] ment, [D] love, and [A] plea –
[D] sure!

[D] Ae fond kiss, [G]and [D] then we [Bm] sever;
[G] Ae fareweel, a- [A] las, for [D] ever!
[G] Deep in heart-wrung [D] tears I'll [Bm] pledge thee,
[D] War – [A7] ring [D] sighs [G] and [D] groans I'll [A] wage
[D] thee!

D
G
A
Bm
A7

Ae Fond Kiss

D G D A Bm G
Ae fond kiss, and then we se - ver; Ae fare-weel, a -
2 2 5 7 3 2 4 3 7 7 10 7
H
A D G Bm
las, for e- ver! Deep in heart- wrung tears I'll pledge thee,
5 0 2 5 3 7 10 3 3 2 4 3
D A7 D G D A D
Wa- rring sighs and groans I'll wage thee!
2 0 2 7 5 2 0 3

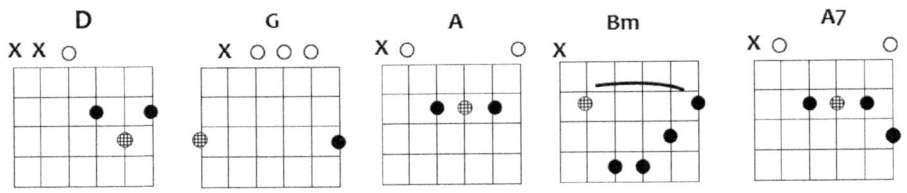

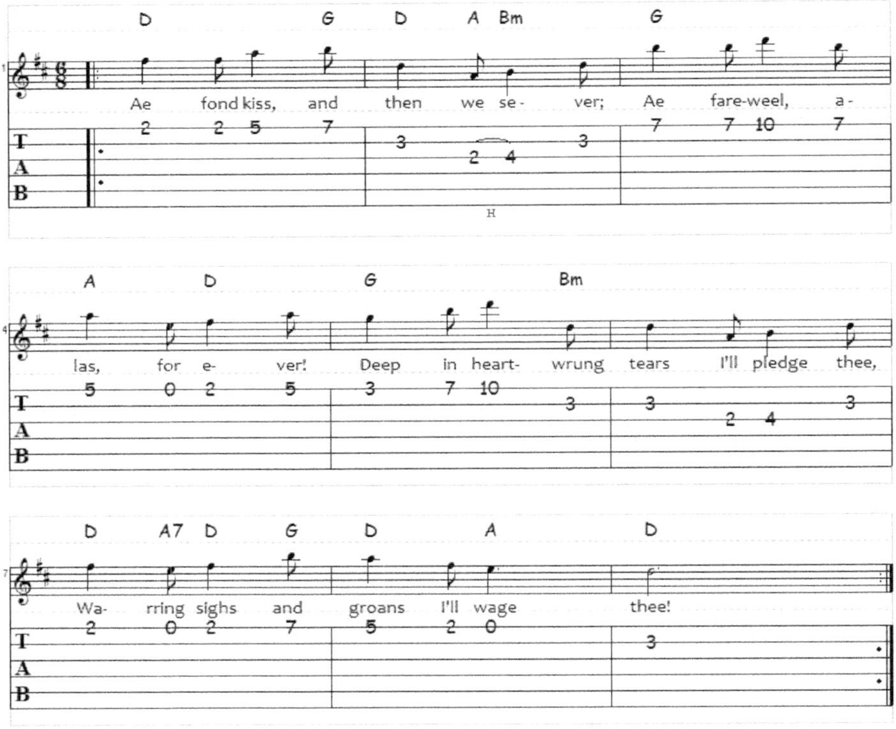

Ae Fond Kiss
Chord Melody

Green Grow the Rashes O (Key D)

Chorus:
[D] Green grow the rashes, O!
[Em] Green grow the rashes, O!
The [G] sweetest hours that [D] e'er I spend
Are [Em] spent amang the [G] lasses, O.

There's [D] nought but care on ev'ry han',
In [Em] every hour that passes, O:
What [G] signifies the [D] life o' man,
An' [Em] 'twere na for the [G] lasses, O.

The [D] warly race may riches chase,
An' [Em] riches still may fly them, O;
An' [G] tho' at last they [D] catch them fast,
Their [Em] hearts can ne'er en – [G] joy them, O.

But [D] gie me a canny hour at e'en,
My [Em] arms about my dearie, O;
An' [G] warly cares, an' [D] warly men,
May [Em] a' gae tapsal – [G] teerie, O.

For [D] you sae douce, ye sneer at this,
Ye're [Em] nought but senseless asses, O:
The [G] wisest man the warl' [D] e'er saw,
He [Em] dearly lov'd the [G] lasses, O.

Auld [D] Nature swears the lovely dears
Her [Em] noblest work she classes, O:
Her [G] 'prentice han' she [D] try'd on man,
An' [Em] then she made the [G] lasses, O.

[repeat Chorus]

The Songs Arranged for Guitar

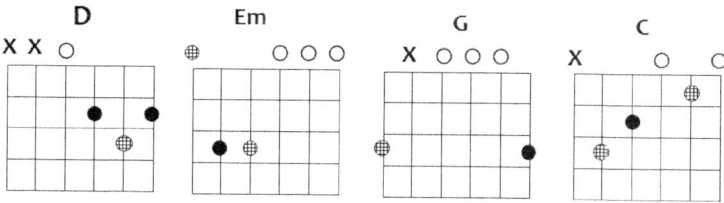

Green Grow the Rashes O

Green Grow the Rashes O
Chord Melody

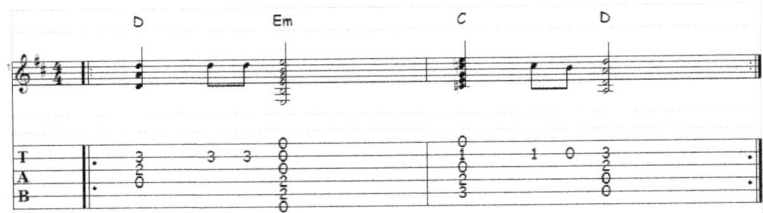

The above can be played as an introduction, after every chorus and as an outro.

Comin' Thro' the Rye (Key D)

[D] Comin thro' the [Em] rye, poor body,
[D] Comin [A7] thro' the [D] rye,
She draigl't a' her [G] petti – [A] coattie,
[D] Comin [A7] thro' the [D] rye!

Chorus :
O, [D] Jenny's a' [G] weet, poor [A] body,
[D] Jenny's [D7] seldom [G] dry;
She [D] draigl't [A7] a' her [D] petti – [A] coattie,
[G] Comin [A7] thro' the [D] rye!

[D] Gin a body [Em] meet a body
[D] Comin [A7] thro' the [D] rye,
Gin a body [G] kiss a [A] body,
[D] Need a [A7] body [D] cry?

Repeat Chorus

[D] Gin a body [Em] meet a body
[D] Comin [A7] thro' the [D] glen,
Gin a body [G] kiss a [A] body,
[D] Need the [A7] warld [D] ken?

Repeat Chorus

[D] Gin a body [Em] meet a body
[D] Comin [A7] thro' the [D] grain;
Gin a body [G] kiss a [A] body,
[D] The thing's a [A7] body's [D] ain.

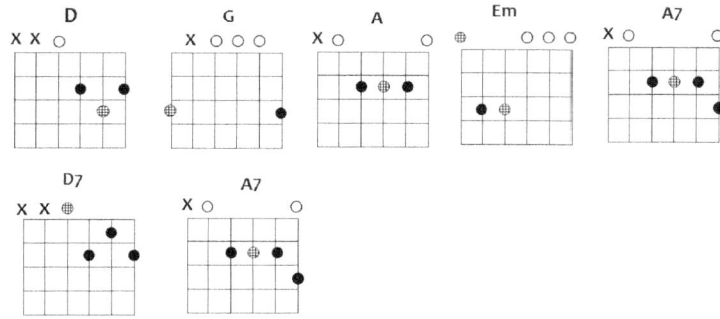

Note: as with many folk songs there are several different versions. The version above appears to be the most true to Burns' version and is often performed. It uses the first verse of the Burns lyric ('O, Jenny's a' weet...') as the chorus, and begins with Burns' second verse.

Comin' Thro' the Rye

The Songs Arranged for Guitar

Comin' Thro' the Rye Chord Melody

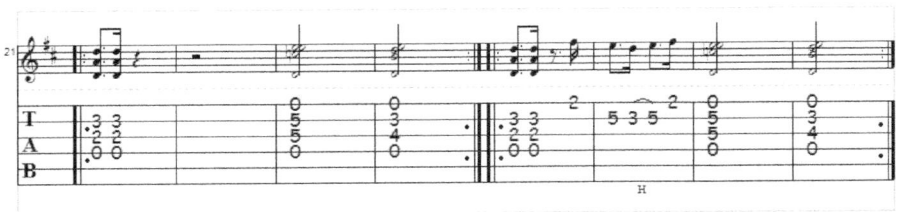

Performance Notes: the first four bars are an introduction, creating a pulse that repeats throughout the song. The spaces can be filled by muting the strings with the left hand and using up and down strokes with the right hand index finger or thumb to imitate a drum beat.

In bar 15 it sounds good if you slow down and this gives you time to play the first beat of bar 16 with emphasis, then a slight pause and you are off on a gallop again!

The last line of music (8 bars and a final bar) are variations on the introduction and are optional – they can be played as an outro or as a vamp between the verses.

This is probably the most technically challenging arrangement in the collection and you can see it on my YouTube channel (Performance and tutorial):

https://www.youtube.com/playlist?list=PLzqwFChU0wVnYg FHgNZJJDtnD2aa7doD4

Easier than typing out the link:
Open **YouTube**.
In the Search Box, type, **'ukulele beginner to brilliant'** (the name of my channel).
Open my channel.
Open the Playlists.
Select the Playlist, **'BURNS – GUITAR EDITION'**.

Scots Wha Hae (Key D)

[D] 'Scots, wha [A7] hae wi [D] Wallace bled,
[G]Scots, wham Bruce has aften led,
[D] Welcome [F#7] tae yer [Bm] gory [F#7] bed,
[Bm] Or tae [G] victo [D] rie. [A7]

[D] 'Now's the day, an now's the hour:
[A] See the [E7] front o [A] battle [A7] **lour**,
[D] See a – [F#7]pproach proud [Bm] Ed–[F#7] ward's power –
[G] Chains and Slave–[D] rie. [A7]

[D] 'Wha will be a [A7] traitor [D] knave?
[G] Wha will fill a coward's grave?
[D] Wha sae [F#7] base as [Bm] be a [F#7] slave?
[Bm] Let him[G] turn an [D] flee. [A7]

[D] 'Wha, for Scotland's king and law,
[A] Freedom's [E7]sword will [A] strongly [A7]draw,
[D] Freeman [F#7] stand, or [Bm] Freeman [F#7] fa,
[G] Let him on wi [D] me.[A7]

[D] 'By Oppression's [A7] woes and [D] pains,
[G] By your sons in servile chains!
[D] We will [F#7] drain our [Bm] dearest [F#7] veins,
[Bm] But they [G] shall be [D] free. [A7]

[D] 'Lay the proud usurpers low,
[A] Tyrants [E7] fall in [A] every [A7] foe,
[D] Liberty's [F#7] in [Bm] every [F#7] blow! –
[G] Let us do or [D] dee.

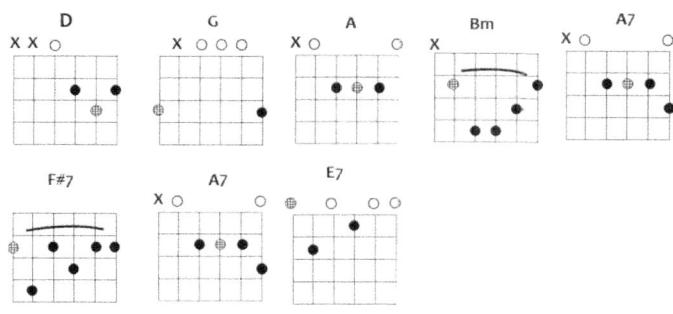

Scots Wha Hae

Scots Wha Hae
Chord Melody

Charlie, He's My Darling (Key Gm)

'Twas [D] on a Monday [Gm] morning,
Right [D] early in the [Gm] year,
That [Eb] Charlie came [Bb] to our town,
The [Cm] young [Gm] Cheva – [D] lier.

CHORUS: An' [Gm] Charlie, he's my darling,
My [Cm] darling, my [Gm] darling,
[Gm] Charlie, he's my dar – [Cm] ling,
The [Gm] young [D7] Cheva – [Gm] lier.

As [D] he was walking [Gm] up the street,
The [D] city for to [Gm] view,
O [Eb] there he spied a [Bb] bonie lass
The [Cm] window [Gm] looking [D] through,

CHORUS

Sae [D] light's he jumped [Gm] up the stair,
And [D] tirl'd at the [Gm] pin;
And [Eb] wha sae ready [Bb] as hersel'
To [Cm] let the [Gm] laddie [D] in.

CHORUS

He [D] set his Jenny [Gm] on his knee,
All [D] in his Highland [Gm] dress;
For [Eb] brawly weel he [Bb] ken'd the way
To [Cm] please a [Gm] bonnie [D] lass.

CHORUS

It's [D] up yon heathery [Gm] mountain,
An' [D] down yon scroggie [Gm] glen,
We [Eb] daur na gang a [Bb] milking,
For [Cm] Charlie [Gm] and his [D] men,

CHORUS

The Songs Arranged for Guitar

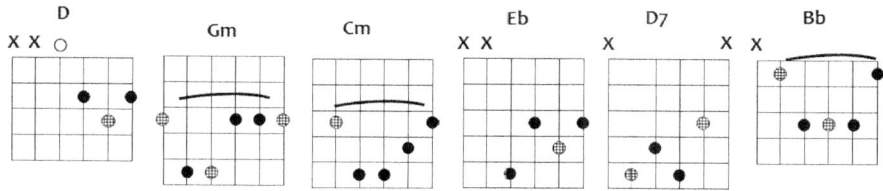

Charlie, He's My Darling

'Twas on a Monday morning, Right early in the year, That Charlie came to our town, The young Chevalier. An' Charlie, he's my darling, My darling, my darling, Charlie, he's my darling, The young Chevalier.

Charlie, He's My Darling Chord Melody

The Songs Arranged for Guitar

Ye Jacobites by Name (Key Em)

When the song is performed, I have noticed singers prefer 'lend an ear' rather than 'give an ear'. Also, the last line and a half of every verse is repeated (as shown below):

Ye (Em) Jacobites by name, give an (G) ear, give an (D) ear,
Ye (Em) Jacobites by (Bm) name, give an (Em) ear;
(D) Ye (G) Jacobites by name,
Your (D) fautes I will proclaim,
Your (Em) doctrines I maun (Bm) blame - you shall (Em) hear!
You shall (D) hear!
 Your (Em) doctrines I maun (Bm) blame - you shall (Em) hear!

What is (Em) Right and what is Wrang, by the (G) law, by the (D) law?
What is (Em) Right and what is (Bm) Wrang by the (Em) law?
What (D) is (G) Right, and what is Wrang?
A (D) short sword, and a lang,
A (Em) weak arm and a (Bm) strang, for to (Em) draw! For to (D) draw!
A (Em) weak arm and a (Bm) strang, for to (Em) draw!

What (Em) makes heroic strife, famed a-(G) far, famed a- (D) far?
What (Em) makes heroic (Bm) strife famed a- (Em) far?
(D) What (G) makes heroic strife?
To (D) whet th' Assassin's knife,
Or (Em) haunt a Parent's (Bm) life, wi' bluidy (Em) war, wi' bluidy (D) war?
Or (Em) haunt a Parent's (Bm) life, wi' bluidy (Em) war?

Then (Em) let your schemes alone, in the (G) State, in the (D) State,
Then (Em) let your schemes a- (Bm) lone in the (Em) state.
(D) Then (G) let your schemes alone,
A- (D) dore the rising sun,
And (Em) leave a man un- (Bm) done, to his (Em) fate, to his (D) fate
And (Em) leave a man un- (Bm) done, to his (Em) fate.

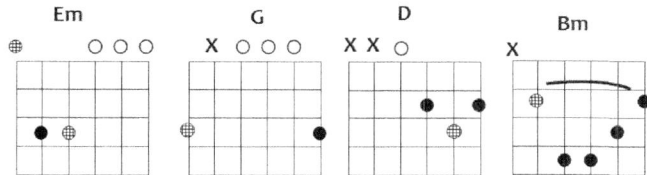

Ye Jacobites by Name

Ye Jacobites by Name Chord Melody

A Man's a Man for A' That (Key E)

Is [E] there, for honest [A] poverty
That [E] hangs his head, and [A] a' that;
The [E] coward slave, we [A] pass him by,
We [E] dare be [A] poor for [B7] a' that!
For [E] a' that, and [F#m] a' that,
Our [E] toils obscure, and [A] a' that,
The [E] rank is but the [F#m] guinea's stamp,
The [E] Man's the [A] gowd for [B7] a' that.

What [E] though on hamely [A] fare we dine,
Wear [E] hoddin gray, and [A] a' that;
Gie [E] fools their silks, and [A] knaves their wine,
A [E] man's a [A] man, for [B7] a' that!
For [E] a' that, and [F#m] a' that,
Their [E] tinsel show, and [A] a' that;
The [E] honest man, though [F#m] e'er sae poor,
Is [E] king o' [A] men for [B7] a' that!

Ye [E] see yon birkie, [A] ca'd a lord,
Wha [E] struts, and stares, and [A] a' that;
Though [E] hundreds worship [A] at his word,
He's [E] but a [A] coof for [B7] a' that.
For [E] a' that, and [F#m] a' that,
His [E] riband, star, and [A] a' that,
The [E] man of inde – [F#m] pendent mind,
He [E] looks and [A] laughs at [B7] a' that.

A [E] king can make a [A] belted knight,
A [E] marquis, duke, and [A] a' that,
But an [E] honest man's a – [A] boon his might,
Guid [E] faith, he [A] maunna [B7] fa' that!
For [E] a' that, and [F#m] a' that,
Their [E] dignities, and [A] a' that,
The [E] pith o' sense, and [F#m] pride o' worth,
Are [E] higher [A] ranks than [B7] a' that.

Then [E] let us pray that [A] come it may -
As [E] come it will for [A] a' that -
That [E] sense and worth, o'er [A] a' the earth,

May [E] bear the [A] gree, and [B7] a' that;
For [E] a' that, and [F#m] a' that,
It's [E] coming yet for [A] a' that,
That [E] man to man, the [F#m] world o'er,
Shall [E] brothers [A] be for [B7] a' that!

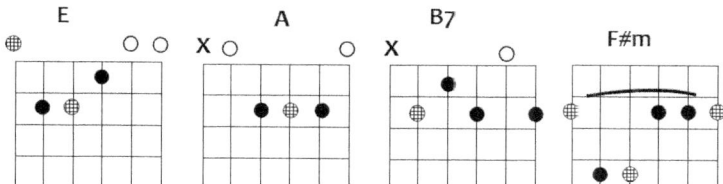

A Man's a Man for A' That

A Man's a Man for A' That Chord melody

outro:

A Man's a Man for A' That (Key D)

Is [D] there, for honest [G] poverty
That [D] hangs his head, and [G] a' that;
The [D] coward slave, we [G] pass him by,
We [D] dare be [G] poor for [A7] a' that!
For [D] a' that, and [Em] a' that,
Our [D] toils obscure, and [G] a' that,
The [D] rank is but the [Em] guinea's stamp,
The [D] Man's the [G] gowd for [A7] a' that.

What [D] though on hamely [G] fare we dine,
Wear [D] hoddin gray, and [G] a' that;
Gie [D] fools their silks, and [G] knaves their wine,
A [D] man's a [G] man, for [A7] a' that!
For [D] a' that, and [Em] a' that,
Their [D] tinsel show, and [G] a' that;
The [D] honest man, though [Em] e'er sae poor,
Is [D] king o' [G] men for [A7] a' that!

Ye [D] see yon birkie, [G] ca'd a lord,
Wha [D] struts, and stares, and [G] a' that;
Though [D] hundreds worship [G] at his word,
He's [D] but a [G] coof for [A7] a' that.
For [D] a' that, and[Em] a' that,
His [D] riband, star, and [G] a' that,
The [D] man of inde – [Em] pendent mind,
He [D] looks and [G] laughs at [A7] a' that.

A [D] king can make a [G] belted knight,
A [D] marquis, duke, and [G] a' that,
But an [D] honest man's a – [G] boon his might,
Guid [D] faith, he [G] maunna [A7] fa' that!
For [D] a' that, and [Em] a' that,
Their [D] dignities, and [G] a' that,
The [D] pith o' sense, and [Em] pride o' worth,
Are [D] higher [G] ranks than [A7] a' that.

Then [D] let us pray that [G] come it may -
As [D] come it will for [G] a' that -
That [D] sense and worth, o'er [G] a' the earth,
May [D] bear the [G] gree, and [A7] a' that;
For [D] a' that, and [Em] a' that,
It's [D] coming yet for [G] a' that,
That [D] man to man, the [Em] world o'er,
Shall [D] brothers [G] be for[A7] a' that!

The Songs Arranged for Guitar

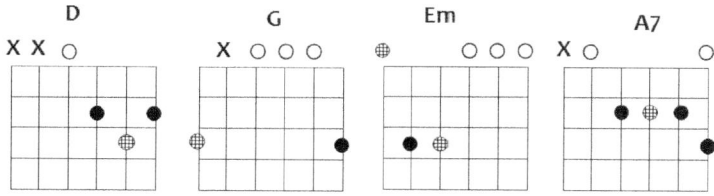

A Man's a Man for A' That

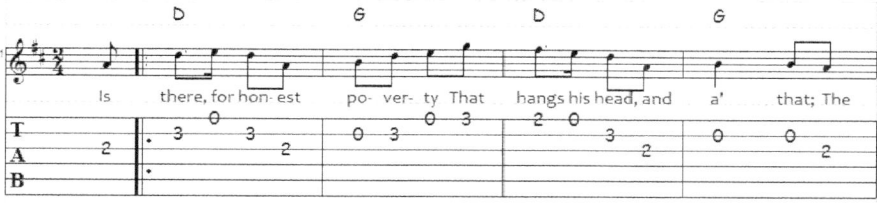
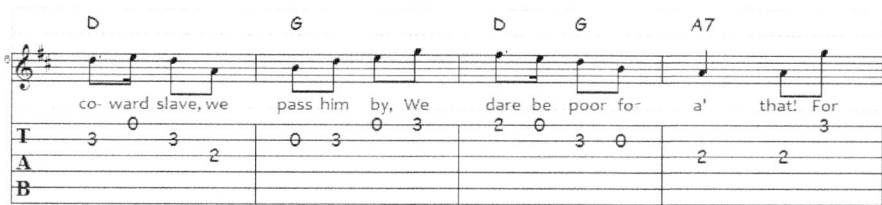
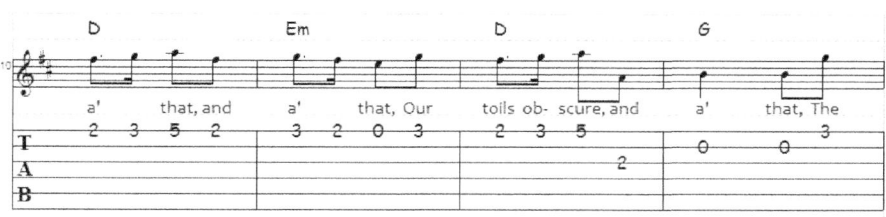
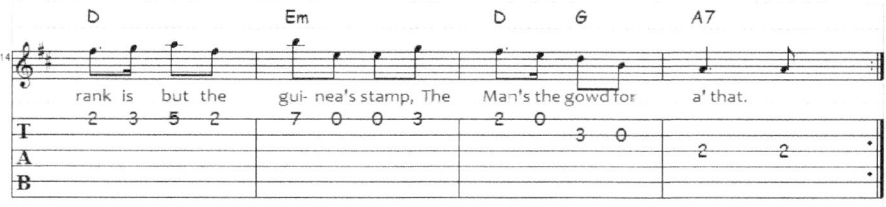

A Man's a Man for A' That Chord Melody

Note: play alternating bars of D and G for an intro, outro, or between verses

Auld Lang Syne (Key D)

Should [D] auld acquaintance [A] be forgot,
And [D] never brought to [G] min'?
Should [D] auld acquaintance [A] be forgot,
And [G] auld lang [D] syne?

Chorus
[G] For [D] auld lang [A] syne, my dear,
[G] For [D] auld lang [G] syne,
We'll [D] tak a cup 0' [A] kindness yet,
For [G] auld lang [D] syne.

We [D] twa hae run a – [A] bout the braes
And [D] pu'd the gowans [G] fine;
But we've [D] wandered mony a [A] weary fit
Sin' [G] auld lang [D] syne.

We [D] twa hae paidl't [A] i 'the burn,
Frae [D] mornin' sun till [G] dine;
But [D] seas between us [A] braid hae roar'd
Sin'[G] auld lang [D] syne...

Repeat Chorus

And [D] surely ye'll be your [A] pint stowp
And [D] surely I'll be [G] mine!
And we'll [D] tak a cup 0' [A] kindness yet,
For [G] auld lang [D] syne.

And [D] there's a hand, my [A] trusty fiere!
And [D] gie's a hand 0' [G] thine!
And we'll [D] *tak* a right guid-[A] willie-waught,
For [G] auld lang [D] syne.

Repeat Chorus

Notes: The verses and choruses can be rearranged. Dougie Maclean performs them in the order shown above. Eddi Reader's album version is similar, only she puts the chorus after the first, fourth and last verses. Also, many singers expand the last line (verse or chorus) to 'for the days of auld lang syne'; or to 'for the sake of auld lang syne'. To end the song, you can repeat the whole chorus or, hit a C chord before repeating the last two lines of the chorus.

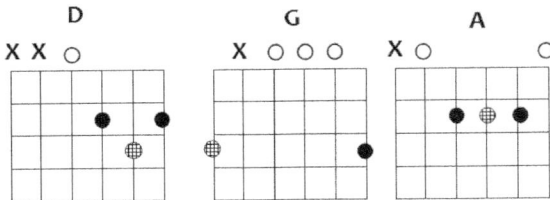

Auld Lang Syne

Auld Lang Syne Chord Melody

Auld Lang Syne Chord Melody
(using D major scale harmonised in thirds)

continued next page...

BURNS

Postscript

There is much I have left out or sketched over in my desire to focus on certain events, ideas or themes. For a more detailed account of Robert Burns' life I recommend the books in the Bibliography - any and all of them.

I've tried to make this book as accurate as possible and cross referenced many of the details, finding quite a few discrepancies and disagreements (as you might expect from biographers tackling the subject over a span of two hundred years).

Despite its failings and eccentricities, I hope this has been an entertaining and welcome addition to the hundreds (perhaps thousands) of books already written about Scotland's greatest poet.

If you enjoyed this book then please leave a star rating and short review on Amazon.

I perform the chord melody arrangements of all 12 songs on **YouTube** and some performances are followed up with a tutorial. The videos can be accessed through this link:

https://www.youtube.com/playlist?list=PLzqwFChU0wVnYgFHgNZJJDtnD2aa7doD4

Alternatively, open **YouTube**.
In the Search Box, type, **'ukulele beginner to brilliant'** (the name of my channel).
Open my channel.
Open the Playlists.
Select the Playlist, **'BURNS – GUITAR EDITION'**.
Subscribe and feel free to ask questions in the Comments Section - I will respond.

I have also released a version of this book for ukulele. The text is identical, only the arrangements differ.

Goodbye, good luck, and lang may yer lum reek,

    Douglas Robert Falconer
    (Benfleet, England, 9th December, 2020)

Bibliography

I used numerous resources, cross referencing biographical details of Robert Burns life as well as the songs and the interpretations to make this book as accurate as possible.

Burnett, Allan (2007) **Robert Burns And All That** (Birlinn Limited)
- a quick, easy read – illustrated and suitable for children

Grimble, Ian (1994) **Robert Burns** (Lomond Books)
- my favourite book, it manages to combine brevity, depth, and fine photographs of Burns' world and its inhabitants

Other resources (in alphabetical order by author surname)

Carswell, Catherine (1930) **The Life of Robert Burns** (Canongate Classics)

Crawford, Robert (2009) **The Bard: Robert Burns, a Biography** (Jonathan Cape)

McIntyre, Ian (2009) **Robert Burns A Life** (Constable)

Mackie, Allister (2019) **Robert Burns: Warts and all A Brief but Honest Exploration of Scotland's Bard** (eBook)

Wilkie, George Scott (2002) **Understanding Robert Burns: verse, explanation and glossary** (Neil Wilson Publishing Limited – Glasgow)

Also
The Complete Poems and Songs of Robert Burns (Geddes and Grosset) (2000)

de Bolla, P. Leask, N. Simpson, D. (2005) **Land, Nation, and Culture 1740-1840** (Palgrave Macmillan, London) - Chapter 10, 'Burns, Wordsworth and the Politics of Vernacular Poetry'.

Tillyard E M (1942) **The Elizabethan World Picture**

Online Resources

(please bear in mind that over time these sites can disappear and links become invalid)

Robert Burns, **The Merry Muses of Caledonia**
https://archive.org/stream/merrymusesofcaleburn/merrymusesofcaleburn_djvu.txt or
https://archive.org/details/merrymusesofcaleburn

Poems: http://www.bbc.co.uk/arts/robertburns/works/

Sylvander and Clarinda correspondence:
https://burnsletters.wordpress.com/category/clarinda/

'Battle of Bannockburn: What was it all about?' by Andrew Black (24th June 2014) https://www.bbc.co.uk/news/uk-scotland-27900285

Scottish History online:
http://scotshistoryonline.co.uk/charlieb.html

W W Knox, A History of the Scottish People – The Scottish Educational System 1840 to 1940
https://www.scran.ac.uk/scotland/pdf/SP2_1Education.pdf

Appendix 1

In 1780 the sum of £1, 200 gave you the purchasing power to buy any one of the following: 114 horses; 240 cows; 1333 stones of wool; 210 quarters of wheat; or pay the wages of a skilled tradesman for 8000 days.
https://www.nationalarchives.gov.uk/currency-converter/#currency-result

Now, imagining a skilled tradesman works 250 days a year (taking weekends and a mere 11 days off for holidays), 8000 days equates to 32 years. Today, in 2020, a skilled tradesman earns at least £50,000 a year but let us assume a much lower sum of £30,000 p.a. to give us a conservative estimate of: 32 x £30,000 = £960, 000. This is at wide variance with the national archives calculation. So, £1,200 in Burns' day could have been worth as little as £52, 887.48 but, in terms of real purchasing power, was closer to a million pounds.

Here are three different methods of calculating today's value for money in Burns' time (1780). None are right or wrong – it is very problematical to compare money over time. Society was different then, people were generally much poorer, but then they didn't have cars, washing machines, televisions, mobile phones or a host of other junk with built in obsolescence to buy and keep renewing for the rest of their lives!

1. Bank of England calculator:
https://www.bankofengland.co.uk/monetary-policy/inflation/inflation-calculator
'What would goods and services costing **£1** in 1780 cost in 2019? The answer the Bank of England online calculator gives is **£180.84**
- which is achieved by multiplying £1 by 180. In a sense this is absurd. If an unskilled worker in 1780 earned £10 a year then if

you paid him £1 you would get more than a month's work out of him. However, there is no way you would get a modern UK worker to work for a month for £180.84! The UK minimum wage today is £8.72 an hour for over 25's; £8.20 for 21 to 24 year olds; £6.45 for 18 to 20's; £4.55 for under 18's; and £4.15 for apprentices.   https://www.gov.uk/national-minimum-wage-rates

Even if we take the lowest possible hourly rate of £4.15 and multiply it by 40 (for a 40 hour working week) we arrive at a wage of £166 per week. This suggests the Bank of England calculation is out by a multiple of around 4 – at the very least – so that would give us 4 x 180 = 720. So by this method £1 in 1780 would be worth £720 today – **a multiple of 720.**

2. Mackie's calculation in Ch.1 is based on an unskilled farm labourer's wage of **£5** in 1786 being compared to an equivalent wage of **£12,500** in 2017. So, **a multiple of 2500.**

3. My method: the Bank of England conversion (x 180 or my adjusted version of x 720) seems far too low and Mackie's (x 2500) too high. So, my approach is to take the average worker's wage in 1780 as **£10 per annum** and compare it with an unskilled or semi-skilled salary in 2020's Britain, which would be around **£15, 000**. This gives us an answer that is, I hope, more accurate i.e. **a multiple of 1,500.**

For American readers, to convert £1 today to the US dollar, just multiply £1 by 1.29.
   For Canadian dollars, multiply £1 by 1.7.
   For European readers multiply £1 by 1.115 for the value in Euros.

Appendix 2
Burns' children

Burns had twelve children (that we know of). Many of them died in childhood. I found it difficult to keep track of them so here they are with their birth and death years:

Elizabeth Paton Burns 1785 - 1817 (with Elizabeth Paton)
Jean Armour Burns 1786 - Died 11 Months, twin to Robert (with Jean Armour)
Robert Burns 1786-1857, twin to Jean (with Jean Armour)
Robert (Clow) 1788 - ? (with Jenny Clow)
Twin Girls 1788 Died within a month of being born (with Jean Armour)
Francis Wallace Burns 1789 - 1803(with Jean Armour)
Elizabeth Park Burns 1791 - 1873 (with Ann Park)
William Nicol Burns 1791 - 1872 (with Jean Armour)
Elizabeth Riddell Burns 1792 - 1795 (with Jean Armour)
James Glencairn Burns 1794 - 1865 (with Jean Armour)
Maxwell Burns 1796 - 1799 (with Jean Armour)

Appendix 3
Important Dates

1305 William Wallace executed in London
1314 The Battle of Bannockburn: Robert the Bruce defeats the English army of King Edward II. celebrated in 'Scots Wha Hae'.
1320 Scottish Independence – The Declaration of Arbroath.
1328 Treaty of Northampton – England recognises Scottish Independence.
1534 Henry VIII sets up the Church of England so he can divorce Catherine of Aragon. He declares himself the Supreme Head of the Church of England.
1603 The Union of Crowns: James VI of Scotland is crowned James I of England - the first king to rule over both countries.
1620 The Pilgrim Fathers sail, on The Mayflower, from Plymouth in Devon to America.
1642 English Civil War between Parliamentarian 'Roundheads' and Royalist 'Cavaliers'.
1649 King Charles I is executed.
1653 Oliver Cromwell becomes 'Lord Protector'.
1658 Cromwell dies.
1660 The Monarchy is restored with King Charles II.
1685 James II, a Catholic, is crowned.
1688 Revolt against James II. He flees to France and dies in 1701.
1689 James II's daughter Mary rules jointly with her Dutch husband William of Orange.
1696 The Scottish Education Act ordains a school in every parish in Scotland.
1702 Queen Anne's reign begins.
1707 The Act of Union (unites the kingdoms of Scotland and England). Robert Burns recalls this event in 'A Parcel O'Rogues'.
1715 Jacobite rebellion (to restore the Stuart line with King James III).
1727 King George II - reigns until 1760.
1745 Jacobite rebellion led by Bonnie Prince Charlie, culminating in defeat for the Scots at the Battle of Culloden in 1746.

1759 **Robert Burns born** to Agnes Broun and William Burness in Alloway, on the 25th January (brothers and sisters, Gilbert, William, John, Agnes, Annabella, and Isobel to follow).

Appendix 3: Important Dates

1760 King George III - reigns until 1820.
1765 Robert attends William Campbell school and is then privately tutored by John Murdoch.
1776 the Burns family moves to Mount Oliphant farm, southeast of Alloway.
1768 Tutor Murdoch leaves. William Burness continues to teach Robert and Gilbert.
1769 Murdoch returns for a spell.
1773 Robert goes to Ayr to study grammar, French and Latin with Murdoch.
1774 Harvesting with Nelly Kirkpatrick. Robert's first innocent love inspires his first song.
1775 Maths summer school in Kirkoswald with Hugh Rodger. Peggy Thomson (13), Robert's second innocent love.
1776 **American Declaration of Independence from Britain.** The two countries are at war until 1783.
1777 The Burns family move to Lochlea Farm near Tarbolton. Robert defies father over attending a dancing school.
1780 The Tarbolton Bachelors' Club is formed.
1781 Robert is sent to Irvine to learn the flax trade and opens a shop. Becomes a Freemason. First serious bout of illness. Befriends worldly sailor Richard Brown.
1782 Burns returns to Lochlea. William in legal dispute with landlord.
1784 The family move to Mossgiel Farm near Mauchline. William Burness dies 13th February, soon after winning his legal case. Family change name to Burns. Servant Elizabeth Paton pregnant by Robert – church censure and public humiliation on the fornicator's stool. Burns meets Jean Armour.
1785 Elizabeth Paton gives birth to a daughter, Elizabeth, on 22nd May. Jean Armour pregnant by Robert and he marries her in a private arrangement. Her parents refuse to acknowledge the union, engage a lawyer to annul the marriage, and send Jean away to stay with a relative. The church investigates. Robert feels betrayed by Jean, and plans to emigrate to Jamaica to work as an Overseer on a sugar plantation. Burns has an affair with Mary Campbell ('Highland Mary').
1786 Mary Campbell may be pregnant by Burns and he may have privately married her too. Perhaps worried about charges of bigamy he asks for and is given a bachelor certificate by the church. Mary dies, possibly while pregnant. **Poems Chiefly in the Scottish Dialect** is

published in Kilmarnock in July. To avoid financial claims for paternity from the Armours, Burns signs all his property and poetry profits over to his brother Gilbert. Burns goes to Edinburgh for a five month stay, to arrange publishing a second edition of his poems. Twins, Robert and Jean Burns, born to Jean Armour.

1787 Edinburgh: May (Margaret/Peggy/Meg) Cameron, a servant, is pregnant by Burns. Joins 'The Crochallan Fencibles'. The bawdy verse is later collected in a volume called, **The Merry Muses of Caledonia**. Robert pays for a headstone for the poet Robert Fergusson. The Edinburgh edition of **Poems Chiefly in the Scottish Dialect** is printed. James Johnson asks Robert to contribute fresh lyrics and to edit and improve old Scots songs for **The Scots Musical Museum**. This becomes Robert's main artistic focus for the rest of his life. Tours the Borders with Robert Ainslie and collects local songs.

He returns home for two weeks, makes Jean pregnant, and is off again for a second tour. Writ from May Cameron. Asks Margaret Chalmers to marry him but is refused. Volume 1 of Johnson's **The Scots Musical Museum** published (with 3 songs by Burns). Meets Agnes McLehose.

1788 Edinburgh: passionate but chaste affair with Agnes (Nancy) McLehose. Wary of scandal they devise the nicknames Clarinda and Sylvander for their flirtatious letters.

Officially marries Jean Armour. Jean has twin daughters but they die within a month of being born. Rents farmland at Ellisland, near Dumfries. On his next return to Edinburgh Burns makes Jenny Clow pregnant. She bears him a son, Robert, and issues a writ for money for his upkeep. Volume 2 of **The Scots Musical Museum** is published (with 35 songs by Burns). Begins work with the Excise.

1789 **The French Revolution** - the fall of the Bastille. Jean moves into Ellisland and has a son, Francis Wallace Burns.

1790 **The Scots Musical Museum**, 3rd edition. Robert adds Jacobite songs, 'My hearts in the Highlands', and 'John Anderson, my Jo'. William Burns, his brother, dies in London. Affair with Ann Park, the Globe Inn landlady in Dumfries. Writes 'Tam o' Shanter' in the autumn. Promoted by the Excise to a foot walk.

1791 In March, Ann Park bears Robert a daughter, Elizabeth (Betty). In April, Jean bears him a son, William Nicol. Robert gives up Ellisland and moves to Dumfries.

Thomas Paine, **The Rights of Man** is published.

Appendix 3: Important Dates

1792 Jean bears a daughter, Elizabeth Riddell Burns. Jenny Clow dies. Writes 'Ae Fond Kiss' for Nancy who sails for Jamaica in January to rejoin her husband. Jean takes in Ann Park's child. **The Scots Musical Museum** 4th edition published (contains 50 songs by Robert Burns), includes 'A Parcel o' Rogues'. Begins work on **A Select Collection of Original Scottish Airs** with George Thomson. Thomas Paine, found guilty of treason. Burns investigated by the Board of Excise for his political views. Promoted to the Dumfries Port Division.

1793 21st January: Louis XVI guillotined. February 1st – France declares war on Britain (war lasted until 1802). A 'Freeman' of Dumfries. Moves to a larger house in Dumfries. Tour of Galloway: writes 'Scots Wha Hae' and 'My Luve is like a Red, Red rose'. Thomson's 1st volume of 25 songs (6 by Burns) published. Befriends Maria Riddell.

1794 Joins Dumfries Volunteer Corps. Jean has another son, James Glencairn Burns.

1795 Burns' 3 year old daughter Elizabeth Riddell Burns dies. Health declines.

1796 Solway bathing cure. Jean pregnant. Visits Maria Riddell asking any requests for the afterlife. Jessy Lewars nurses him. **Dies 21st July.** On the day of the funeral Jean gives birth to her ninth child, Maxwell. Volume 5 of Johnson's **The Scots Musical Museum**, with 37 songs by Burns (including 'Auld Lang Syne').

1798 **Lyrical Ballads** by William Wordsworth and Samuel Taylor Coleridge published - generally viewed as the beginning of the English Romantic movement in literature.

A Short Glossary of Scots Words

aboon above, up, beyond
acquent acquainted
ae one
ain own
auld old
awa' away

bairn child
baith both
beld bald
bide abide endure
birkie lively or conceited fellow
blether talk nonsense
bonnie pretty beautiful
braes steep river banks
brent smooth
braw handsome fine good

ca' call
cannie quiet
cantie lively
Chevalier Cavalier (horseback knight)
clatter gossip
coof a simpleton or fool
cutty short
cutty-stool a small stool used for repentance in church
crummock a cudgel, a crooked staff

daur dare
dochter daughter
douce sedate sober prudent respectable
drouk to wet, to drench
drouthy thirsty
drucken drunken

e'en even; evening

fa' fall
fautes faults
fit foot
fou or **fow** drunk

gang to go
gaunted gaped, yawned
gie give
gloamin twilight
glow'r stare
gowans daisies
gowd, **goud** gold
greet cry

haggis the minced lungs, heart and liver of a sheep, mixed with oatmeal, suet, onions, pepper and salt and cooked in a sheep's stomach
hame home
hauf half
haun hand
havers nonsense
houghmagandie fornication
howlet owl
hurdies buttocks

ilka each, every

jink the slip, an escape
jo sweetheart

keek a look, glance
ken to know
kent known
kintry country

lough a pond, loch or lake
lour threaten

lum chimney
luve love

mair more
maut malt
meikle much, great
midden a dunghill
min' mind, remembrance
mirk dark
monie, mony many

nappy strong ale or drink
ne'er never

oxter armpit

palaver idle talk, nonsense

rair roar
reekit stank

sae so
sairly sorely
scauld scold
scrog a short stunted tree or bush
scroggie abounding in stunted bushes
shank travel on foot
shoon shoes
sic such
skellum scoundrel
skelp to smack
skirl to cry or sing shrilly
sklent a slant, a glance
skyte a slap
sleekit smooth and glossy, crafty, sly
snaw-broo melted snow
snirtle to laugh in a suppressed manner, snigger
souk suck

stour strife, adversity, dust
stowp or stoup drinking vessel
syne ago, since,

tae toe
tappet-hen a bottle in the shape of a hen, holding three quarts of claret
tapsalteerie topsy-turvy, upside-down
targe a shield
tent to attend to
tentless careless
theckit thatched
thegither together
thrapple the windpipe, throat, neck
tinkler a tinker, gypsy
tirl'd rattled
tittlin whispering
tocher a dowry
trews trousers
tyke a dog

unco uncommon, strange, unknown, extremely, very
usquebae whisky

vauntie boastful, proud

wab web
wabster a weaver
waught a big drink
waukin awake
wee small
wham whom

yestreen last night

INDEX

'A Man's a Man for a'That	115-119, 190
'A Parcel O' Rogues'	92-93
'A Poet's Welcome to his Love Begotten Daughter"	34
'Ae Fond Kiss'	56-59, 171
'Age of Aquarius'	16
'Auld Lang Syne'	119-125, 197
'Charlie He's my Darling'	99-101, 184
'Comin' Thro' the Rye'	69-72, 177
'Daffodils'	16
'Flower of Scotland'	81
'Green Grow the Rashes O'	65-69, 174
'Hey Tuttie Tatie'	81
'Holy Willie's Prayer'	15
'John Anderson, My Jo'	23-24, 159
'Kubla Khan'	17
'Leezie Lindsay'	21-22, 156
'My Luve is Like a Red, Red Rose'	50-53, 162
'Nae Hair On't'	63
'On a Bank of Flowers'	17
'Robt Burns The Fornicator'	63
'Scotland the Brave'	81
'Scots Wha Hae'	75-82, 181
'Tam o' Shanter'	130-137
'The Brigs of Ayr'	6
'The Deil's Awa' Wi' Th' Exciseman'	151
'The Wanderer Above the Sea of Fog'	13, 14
'To a Mouse'	xiv
'Woodstock'	16
'Ye Banks and Braes o' Bonnie Doon	54-55, 165
'Ye Jacobites by Name'	102-105, 187

Ainslie, Robert	40, 42,
Antoinette, Marie	129
Aristophanes	141
Armour, Jean	5, 8, 33, 35, 48-50, 129, 140, 142, 145-146
Bachelor's certificate	38
Bain, Ally	69
Bannockburn, The Battle of	76

INDEX

Bastille, Storming of the	129
bawdy	61
BBC Queen Street	122
Begbie, Alison	29
Blacklock, Thomas	40
Blake, William	9, 12, 16, 17
Bonnie Prince Charlie	96-102
(the lost portrait)	96-97
Braveheart	76
Broun, Agnes	27
Brown, Richard	4, 30
brucellosis	147
Buchan, Elizabeth/Elspeth	31
Burness, William	32, 149
Burns, Gilbert	137, 146
Byron, Lord	9, 17
Calvinism (John Knox)	61-62
Cameron, May	41, 43, 44
Campbell, Mary	37-39
Cavaliers	87
Chalmers, Peggy	44
Clow, Jenny	127, 128, 138
cobbles	128
Coleridge, Samuel Taylor	9, 17
Connery, Sean	xiii, 122
Covid 19	144
Creech	41
Crichton-Browne, James	147
Cromwell, Oliver	87
Culloden, The Battle of	98, 105, 106
Cumming, Alan	1
Cunningham, Phil	69
Currie, James	11, 139
cutty stool	33
Dad's Army	62
Defoe, Daniel	111
Deacon Blue	xi
Democracy	112, 113
Dumfries Volunteer Corps	143, 145
Dumfries	11, 49, 127, 129, 130, 137, 138, 141, 143, 144, 146

219

Dylan, Bob	xvii, 50
Edinburgh Military Tattoo	123
Edinburgh	40,
Education	110, 111
Egalitarianism	114, 115
Ellisland	49, 137
endocarditis	147
epitath for William	32
Excise	42, 49, 127, 128, 129, 139
Fawkes, Guy	85-86
Fergusson, Robert	20, 30, 41
flax	29-30
'flower power'	16, 17
Freemasonry	14, 29-30, 40, 137
Friedrich, Caspar David	13
funeral	6, 144, 146
Gardner, Jean	31
Geology	52
George Bernard Shaw	121
Gettysburg Address	115
Gibson, Mel	76
Gow, Neil	43
Grosvenor, Bendor	96
guillotine	114
Habbie stanza	11, 15, 33-35
Hair	16
Hamlet	88
Harrison, Rex	122
Hartley, L P (**The Go-Between**)	36
Hippies	15-17
Hutton, James	52
hypochondria	31, 144
Irvine	4, 30-32
Jacobites	94-106, 148
Jamaica	35, 37-39
Johnson, James	19-21, 127, 139
King Edward I	76
King Edward II	77
King Henry V	81
King Henry VIII	83
King James II and VII	89, 90, 95, 96

INDEX

King James VI	84,
Kirkpatrick, Nelly	28
Laird, Ross	124
Lawrence, D H	28
Lewars, Jessie	145
Lincoln, Abraham	xvii, 115
Longniddry	96
Lorimer, Jean	142
Louis XVI	140,
Macbeth	88
Martin, Willie	87
Mauchline Kirk	33
Maxwell, Doctor William	144
McLehose, Agnes (Nancy, Clarinda)	44-50, 56-58, 108, 109, 138, 141
Milgram, Stanley	37
Miller, Elizabeth	33
Mitchell, Joni	16
Morrison, Jim	16
Mossgiel, Rob	32, 35, 50
Mount Oliphant	28
Mrs Dunlop	142
mum	xiv, 87, 122
My Fair Lady	122
Knox, John	62, 111
Of Mice and Men	xiv
Orwell, George (**1984**)	86
Paine, Thomas (**The Rights of Man**)	114, 140
Park, Ann	140,
Park, Betty	140
Paton, Elizabeth	33
Poems, Chiefly in the Scottish Dialect	2, 4, 19, 20, 39, 41
Prestonpans (Battle of)	96, 102
Puritans	62
Pygmalion	121
Ramsay, Allan (the lost portrait)	96, 97
Reader, Eddi	xi, 202
regicide	88
Republicanism	115
rheumatic fever	147
Riddell, Maria	41, 142, 145

Robert the Bruce	76-82,
Romanticism	9, 12, 14, 56
Roundheads	87, 89, 101
Scott, Sir Walter	149
sedition	37, 82, 92, 93
Shakespeare, William	4, 81, 88,
Sharpe (Bernard Cornwell novels)	108
Sillar, David	28, 29
Simpson, Homer	xiv
Slavery	35, 36
SNP (Scottish National Party)	xiii, 94, 95
Stanford Prison Experiment	37
Star Trek	xii
Steinbeck, John	xiv
Sylvander	45-47, 56
Tarbolton Bachelor Club	29
The Act of Union (1707)	90, 94
The American Declaration of Independence	115
The Awkward Squad	143, 146,
The Crochallan Fencibles	41
The Divine Right of Kings	87, 88
The French Revolution	9, 129, 140,
The Globe Inn, Dumfries	130, 137
The Merry Muses of Caledonia	63
The Rainbow	28
The Scots Musical Museum	18, 20, 69, 71, 92, 127, 129, 139, 150
The Selkirk Grace	19
The Sublime	xi, 12, 14, 16, 17, 56, 68
The Union of the Crowns	84
The White Heather Club	xiii
Thomson, George (**A Select Collection of Scottish Airs**)	81, 139, 142
Thomson, Peggy	28
Tomorrow's World	xiii
Tours	19, 42, 43, 142
Vernacular of the common man	10, 11, 17, 19, 20, 23, 41, 45
Wallace, William	75, 76
warrant	38
William of Orange	90

INDEX

Wordsworth, William	9-11, 16
zeitgeist	9, 113
Zimbardo	37

Printed in Great Britain
by Amazon